I0824168

THE DREAM ATLAS

ALSO BY FIONA COOK

The Wheel of the Year:
An Illustrated Guide to Nature's Rhythms

THE DREAM ATLAS

An Interactive Guide to Dreamwork

FIONA COOK

ILLUSTRATED BY KATHLEEN NEELEY

AMBER LOTUS®

CONTENTS

Introduction vii

Orienting Your Dreamwork xi

Plotting Discoveries xiv

The Dream Journal xv

CYCLE I: BEGINNING 1

- New Moon: Time to Dream 2
- Waxing: Healthy Sleep Practice 5
- Full Moon: Working with the Moon 8
- Waning: The Spectrum of Consciousness 10

Dreaming Journey: Prehistory 12

CYCLE II: WARMING UP 15

- New Moon: Deep Relaxation 16
- Waxing: Mapping Your Waking Life 18
- Full Moon: Strengthening Dream Recall 20
- Waning: The Stuff of Dreams 22

Dreaming Journey: Mesopotamia 24

CYCLE III: THE SENSES 27

- New Moon: Sensory Processing 28
- Waxing: Dreams and Sound 30
- Full Moon: Smell and Taste 33
- Waning: Dreams and Touch 35

Dreaming Journey: Classical Antiquity 38

CYCLE IV: THE SPIRIT 43

- New Moon: Accessing Spiritual Depths 44
- Waxing: Cultivating Ritual 46
- Full Moon: Dream Deities 48
- Waning: Bedside Ambience 50

Dreaming Journey: Religious Perspectives 52

CYCLE V: THE PSYCHE 57

- New Moon: Dream Psychology 58
- Waxing: Dreaming Toward the Collective 60
- Full Moon: The Shadow 63
- Waning: Interpreting Symbols 66

Dreaming Journey: Dreams and Science 69

CYCLE VI: STRANGE EXPERIENCES 73

- New Moon: Thresholds and Boundaries 74
- Waxing: Precognition and Synchronicity 77
- Full Moon: Big Dreams 79
- Waning: Dream Incubation 82

Dreaming Journey: Asia 84

CYCLE VII: DREAMS AND ART 89

- New Moon: Dreams and Creativity 90
- Waxing: Exploring Color 92
- Full Moon: Context and Juxtaposition 94
- Waning: Illustration 96

Dreaming Journey: Africa 98

CYCLE VIII: DREAMS AND WRITING 101

- New Moon: Dreaming in Verse 102
- Waxing: Literary Dreams 104
- Full Moon: The Art of the Manifesto 106
- Waning: Active Imagination 108

Dreaming Journey: The Americas 110

CYCLE IX: BUILDING SKILLS 115

- New Moon: Animal Connection 116
- Waxing: Connecting to Nature 118
- Full Moon: Envisioning 120
- Waning: Translation and Decoding 122

Dreaming Journey: Australia 124

CYCLE X: DREAM PLAY 127

- New Moon: Disrupting Sleep 128
- Waxing: Lucid Dreaming 130
- Full Moon: Control and Surrender 132
- Waning: Dreams and Technology 134

Dreaming Journey: Europe 137

CYCLE XI: DREAM MAGIC 141

- New Moon: Playing with Time 142
- Waxing: Problem-Solving 144
- Full Moon: Dream Spells 146
- Waning: Working with Cycles 148

Dreaming Journey: The Language of Dreams 150

CYCLE XII: DIVING DEEP 153

- New Moon: Childhood Dreams 154
- Waxing: Nightmares 156
- Full Moon: Dreaming the Dead 159
- Waning: The Water Connection 161

Dreaming Journey: Gods and Spirits 163

Concluding Your Journey *168*

BLUE MOON: COLLABORATIVE DREAMING 171

Further Reading *183*

Bibliography *185*

Acknowledgments *186*

About the Author and Illustrator *188*

INTRODUCTION

TO DREAM IS TO SAIL

Oneiro is the Greek word for "dream," *naut* the word for "sailor." Combined, they form ONEIRONAUT: one who navigates a different type of reality, the strange and mysterious sea of the subconscious. The oneironaut is buoyed upon the waves of their dreams and plunges into their depths, later charting each revelation and discovery.

CONSIDER

While we're examining terms—the roots of origin and the tendrils of meaning—we discover that the word *consider*, too, stems from navigation: the Latin *con-*, meaning "with," and *-sidus/sidereal*, meaning "heavenly body" or "constellation." *Consider* comes from sailors looking up at the stars, mapping their routes across seas.

Consideration is a desirable state of mind for dreamwork: To consider something, one is alert and observant while remaining open to fresh insight. Consideration balances action and passivity, dancing between the conscious state of waking and the intuitive qualities of the subconscious.

Like a sailor guided by the stars, *consider* your dreams. Judiciously allow information to reveal itself to you and steer toward a deeper sense of meaning.

Every night, you lie in bed—eyes closed, body paralyzed—and, whether you remember it or not, you travel to imaginary places, witnessing and participating in things that don't exist—can't exist—in so-called real life.

When we wake, our dreams disperse, often vanishing completely, and we forget that other wild and secret realm as our daytime responsibilities take over.

However, the sense of mystery that dreams offer sometimes lingers—a hint of some elusive, deeper meaning, just out of reach. The desire to understand and hold on to the ephemeral truths revealed to us at night is human, timeless. Historically, people have found many ways to integrate dreams into the fabric of their waking reality, and in some cultures, the distinction between dreaming and waking isn't as clearly defined.

THE BOOK AS AN ATLAS

A book is, by its nature, linear, with a first and last page. Words printed in ink on paper: logical, factual, material, definitive. Dreams are none of these things: They are more layered, ephemeral, and **protean** in nature. Dreams want to play hide-and-seek, most of all when you wish to pin them down. They often possess an element of mischief. *Swim in these waters.*

This book is an atlas: a guide and companion as you journey. Like the maps used by voyagers of yore, it is meant to be interactive—more than a silent reference.

WHAT IS A DREAM?

Just as we do regarding life and death, humans have a variety of ideas about dreams—what they are and how we should respond to them. Reflect on your own beliefs, perhaps jotting down your thoughts in a notebook.

The writing doesn't have to be perfect, permanent, or profound: This is a quick exercise intended to encourage exploration of your own thoughts and feelings.

FIRST, ASK YOURSELF: What is dreaming? What is waking life? How are they different?

NEXT, REFLECT ON YOUR PERSONAL HISTORY: What is my relationship with sleep? With dreams?

IMAGINE: What if we made more room for dreams in our lives? What would this look like on a personal level? How might our communities and society look different?

FINALLY: What can I gain by connecting more deeply to my dreams?

Sit with these questions. You might know some of your answers instantly; some might take time to bloom; and others might, like a dream, evolve and morph over time.

In Greek mythology, Proteus was an ancient god of the sea who had the ability to tell the future, but he would shape-shift to avoid having to do so.

As explorer and cartographer, you are encouraged to add to and amend this book as you go. Make it yours. The atlas lays out some historical and mythological context, offering coordinates to begin from, but it's up to you, the dreamer, to navigate your personal route and plot your discoveries along the way.

Together, we will chart through a year of dreaming. You can move methodically, page by page, day by day, or you can pick up your atlas as you feel compelled. If you realize you've fallen off course, find your bearings, recommit, and get back on track—as many times as you need to.

This atlas is a living document, designed to be revisited again and again. Each time you return to its pages, it will offer something new.

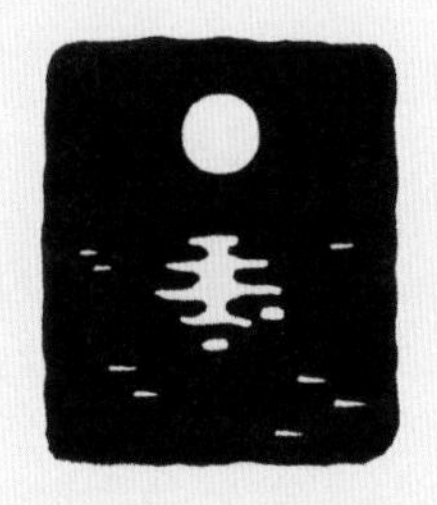

ORIENTING YOUR DREAMWORK

DREAMWORK is the practice of diving deeper into your dreams; getting better at remembering and understanding them; and drawing on them for inspiration, insight, and guidance in your waking life. It's an art built on respecting and honoring dreams, trusting that, like our waking experiences, they are innately valuable and significant.

A NOTE ON STRUCTURE

Since most people tend to sleep at night, this book is structured to align with the phases of the moon. A single moon cycle, from one new moon to the next, is 29.5 days, which means a solar year variably contains either 12 or 13 full moons. (The "extra" 13th moon in a year is known as a "blue moon.") Throughout this year of dreamwork, we'll traverse twelve moon cycles, mirroring the earth's trip around the sun. Each cycle is made up of four weeks, beginning on a new moon and passing through the rhythms of waxing (building), fullness, and waning (letting go) before beginning again.

Each section offers a variety of ways to engage with the concepts of the week. Some exercises are active and hands-on, while others are more reflective, providing food for thought to sit with before bed or even take with you into dreamland.

In between cycles, you'll find stories of how different cultures from around the globe and throughout history have revered, explained, and utilized dreams.

The final offering in this book is an extended collaborative experiment designed to be tried with trusted fellow dreamers: an extra "blue moon," if you will.

Reflect on how these repeating cycles unfold in our waking lives, too, ebbing and flowing as we move through patterns along with our universe.

EXPLORE presents a hands-on challenge.

PLAY inspires you to try something new or think a little differently.

CONSIDER offers concepts to ponder.

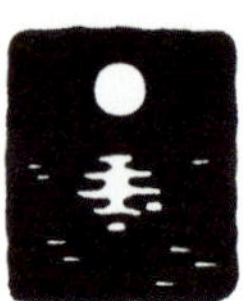

REFLECT invites you to revisit your dream journal entries (or memories) with a specific theme in mind.

CONJURE encourages you to welcome specific themes to your dreams.

CHECK IN serves as a monthly reminder to review your progress.

BEFORE YOU BEGIN

Ahead of any journey, it's important to prepare. In the weeks or days leading up to your first dream cycle, gather the items and information you'll need.

* **LOOK UP WHEN THE NEXT NEW MOON WILL BE, THEN WAIT AND PREPARE FOR THAT DATE.** This intentionality stokes a sense of anticipation and respect that will serve you well.

* **ACQUIRE A NOTEBOOK.** Dub it your "dream journal," and reserve it for recording your dreams, journaling, and completing the exercises and activities in this book.

* **WASH YOUR SHEETS.** To start the cycle with ritual and intention, it's best to have clean sheets and pillowcases on your bed. Have a fresh set ready as you approach the first new moon.

* **GATHER ADDITIONAL SUPPLIES.** As you progress through the book, you'll encounter suggestions for items to use in your practice. Some tools you might gather include:

  * A dream dictionary (see page 66)
  * A bookmark
  * A candle
  * Incense
  * Herbs (suggestions on pages 33 and 119)
  * Essential oils (suggestions on page 34)
  * Sleep- or dream-themed tea
  * Watercolor paints and paintbrush
  * Modeling clay
  * A moon calendar showing the dates of the moon phases. (This can be an app on your phone or a paper calendar.)

PLOTTING DISCOVERIES

As you make your way through this book, keep track of interesting dream experiences in your journal. Jot down the dates they occur and a few notes for reference. Some of the dream experiences on this (non-exhaustive!) list will come about organically, but the list can also suggest types of dreams to seek out.

- A dream within a dream
- Tapping into another's consciousness
- A prophetic dream or "Big Dream" (see page 79)
- Dreaming about or with the dead (a visitation)
- Realizing you're dreaming while asleep
- Feeling physical pain or pleasure in a dream
- Experiencing smell or taste in a dream
- A recurring dream
- A spiritual or divine encounter
- Solving a personal problem or riddle
- Resuming a dream after waking from it
- Seeing your face in a mirror or observing your hands
- Precognitive synchronicity (page 77)
- A meaningful message in a dream
- A hypnagogic experience (page 74)
- A clairsentient experience (page 37)
- Successful dream incubation (page 82)
- Mindful control of a dream (page 132)
- A dream that results in a new or changed understanding of reality
- Dreaming from the perspective of your child-self
- Dreaming from an animal's perspective

THE DREAM JOURNAL

The key to dream recall is actually quite simple: Dedicate time and attention to your dreams. One of the best ways to do this is by writing them down.

Beyond helping with recall, documenting your dreams in writing creates a trove of material you can return to later. You can use your dream journal to look for patterns, seek personal guidance, find creative inspiration, and more.

AN ANCIENT ART

Thousands of years ago, the Mesopotamians chiseled images of their dreams into wet clay to preserve them. Likewise, Synesius, a fifth-century Greek bishop from Cyrene (modern-day Libya) called dreams "personal oracles" and extolled the benefits of keeping a "Night Book"—a dream journal. This advice stands: Documenting our dreams is the best way we have to remember them, understand them, and use them to learn about ourselves.

JOURNALING TIPS

Consider these tips for a fulfilling dream-journaling practice.

* **DON'T DELAY.** When you wake from a dream, its details still fresh in your mind, you may assume you'll remember it later. Sadly, this is almost never true. Get in the habit of recording your dreams as soon as you wake. Even if a dream seems silly or trivial, write it down. Its meaning may take time to emerge.

Keep your dream journal close at hand—under your pillow, for example, or on your bedside table—with a pen beside it. Alternatively, tuck your pen inside your journal, or use a bookmark to keep your place. The less effort it takes to find your journal and open it to the right page, the more likely you'll be to use it.

* **DROP HINTS.** Before you go to sleep, write a few notes about your day at the top of your journal page. This practice not only provides context for future reflections but also encourages a dialogue between your waking and dreaming selves—a harmonious call-and-response.

* **DATE YOUR ENTRIES.** Always record the date—this will make it easier to notice when dreams coincide with significant events (holidays, seasonal shifts, or other celestial occurrences).

Throughout your dreamwork, it might be helpful to pay attention to zodiacal movements—more on page 148.

* **KEEP IT SIMPLE.** You don't need to write much, especially if it's the middle of the night. You also don't have to write neatly or make sense. You don't even have to open your eyes. Try jotting down a few keywords to flesh out later. A fragment, a phrase, even an image, can be surprisingly evocative by daylight.

As dream journaling becomes a habit, you'll remember more and more details upon waking. Remember that you don't need to write everything down. Just note the most vivid images or themes.

* **ASK WHAT, NOT WHY.** Resist analyzing your dreams right away. Instead, focus on the content of the dream—the who, what, where, and when. Write in the present tense to help yourself remember. Pay special attention to any sensory details: What do you see, hear, smell, feel, or taste?

Sometimes, we go through dreaming dry spells, when we can't remember our dreams for nights at a time. When this happens, simply write it in your journal: "Can't remember any dreams." Make a few notes about your quality of sleep instead. Was it a hot night and you tossed and turned? Did you sleep deeply, or were you up often, feeling anxious?

* **BE PATIENT.** The sleepy mind is not the best judge of what is useful or sensible. Try to withhold judgment, and stay with the dream. Not all dreams have profound deeper meanings, but recording imagery and themes can reveal patterns and inspire creativity over time.

Leave a blank space after each dream entry for later notes about what the dream might mean, what memories it triggers, or the ideas it inspires. Use a different-color ink for these additions.

Think of your mind as an overgrown meadow. If you walk the same route through the meadow repeatedly, you'll eventually clear a path.

Writing in your dream journal regularly is like treading a private path toward dreamland. The more you walk it, the more defined the path becomes, and the easier it is to arrive at your destination.

* **DON'T STRESS.** Recording your dreams shouldn't feel like a chore. If the practice becomes overwhelming or stressful, relieve some pressure by recording every other day or every few days. (To make the most of this book, try to record at least one dream a week.)

If you fall out of the habit of writing in your dream journal, don't worry about it. Just start again—as often as you need to.

* **DO IT YOUR WAY.** Some people prefer to speak their dreams aloud into a voice recorder. If you can do this without disturbing any co-sleepers, have at it, but consider transcribing your recordings at a later point. The act of writing by hand is linked to memory, and it can be valuable to have a material record of your dreams to hold and page through later.

All tips aside, do what comes naturally to you! There's no right or wrong way to use a dream journal, so don't overthink it.

CYCLE I

BEGINNING

CYCLE I WEEK 1  NEW MOON

TIME TO DREAM

Dreaming is a fact of life, but dreamwork—actively remembering your dreams and using them to your advantage—may feel like a luxury. Who has the time to lie around in the morning thinking about their dreams, much less the patience to write them all down? Yes, dreaming is free, but the time and relaxed mindset required for dreamwork can seem unattainable. From daily responsibilities to our various hungers and urges, life calls loudly, the moment we open our eyes.

When we invest emotionally in the power and value of our dreams, however, a shift can occur. Priorities change. New doors open.

What happens when you allow yourself a few minutes of contemplation before moving on to your daily tasks and responsibilities? By creating a pause, you invite a sense of calm to your mind while also building your powers of intuition and creative thinking. Whether or not your dream strikes you as profound, these skills and qualities will serve you well throughout your day.

REFLECT:

One goal of dreamwork is to connect with your dream-self—the strange, shadowy side of yourself that exists in another realm each night. By getting to know this side of yourself better, you also gain deeper knowledge of who you are in the waking world.

Before beginning, consider your attitude of approach. Some degree of skepticism is understandable. Dreamwork is most helpful, however, if you allow yourself an open mind.

The activities in this book are designed to be achievable without imposing a burden, and most won't take much longer than fifteen minutes—but they do require some effort. Give each a try, even if an assignment doesn't spark interest, even if it sounds weird or a little boring. Consider this an opportunity to think differently, to stretch your routine . . . and, perhaps, to grow.

Simply wanting to dream more and working toward that goal has been shown to increase the duration of REM sleep in the dreamer. You'll see for yourself as you start giving your dreams more attention: You'll become more aware of them, and you'll be able to recall them in greater detail.

EXPLORE:

Put some thought into why, exactly, you want to spend more time with your dreams. Think about what it might take. What obstacles could arise in the course of this adventure?

Open your journal to a clean page. Ask: What brought me to this moment? What do I, personally, hope to gain from working more closely with my dreams?

Begin by brainstorming. There might be a few reasons you want to explore your dreams. Maybe you're just curious. Maybe there's a situation in your life you hope to learn more about, and you think dreams might offer some insight. Maybe you're creatively stuck and looking for inspiration. Perhaps you've had a powerful, unexplainable dream that you'd like to better understand. Or maybe someone gave you this book and you simply want to give it a try.

Once you've written down your reasons for engaging in dreamwork, go back and reread them. Choose one to prioritize. Condense your thought into a single statement, crafting it like a vow: *It will come true.* The more specific your words, the more honed your focus will be.

SAMPLE INTENTIONS

My dreams will show me how to resolve tension in my relationship.

*

My dreams will inspire my artwork.

*

Dreams will guide me to the next phase of my life.

*

My dreams will help me understand my anger.

*

I will use my dreams to heal my childhood trauma.

*

I will connect with the divine through my dreams.

*

My dreams will help me better understand my place in this world.

If you're struggling to come up with the right statement, you can use a generic intention, such as *I will remember my dreams* or *I will dedicate one month to dreamwork.*

On a fresh page of your dream journal, write your intention. Before you fall asleep, take a good long look at it. Tuck your journal under your pillow so your head is resting on it while you sleep.

PLAY:

Write your dream intention on several small strips of paper. Each day this week, find new ways to relate to it by taking a strip and choosing one of the following actions:

* Carry it with you in your pocket or bag.
* Make a little game of hide-and-seek for yourself: Tape your strip in places you'll stumble upon unexpectedly—the bathroom mirror, the inside of the fridge, on the back of your phone case, etc.
* Burn it, watching it dissolve into ash.
* Bury it.
* Give it to a friend.
* Sing it.
* Leave it in a public place for someone else to find.
* Mail it to a random address.
* Eat it.

CONSIDER:

Dreaming is a chance to play, and everyone deserves to play.

GO DEEPER

In the next week, take a few moments each morning to write down a few sentences about what you encountered in your dreams. Or, if a dream wakes you in the middle of the night, jot down a description of what stirred you.

At this point, you don't need to interpret your dreams in any way. Just honor them with a moment's attention, withholding judgment. However, if any messages or meanings come to you upon reflection, write them down.

HINT: *While it's important to take our commitment to dreamwork seriously, dreams, and even sleep, do not respond well to stern demands. Sometimes, when we focus on something with all our might, it eludes us all the more. Approach your dreamwork with a sense of healthy balance—prioritize your commitment, but don't be too hard on yourself if life gets in the way.*

HEALTHY SLEEP PRACTICE

We humans need about eight hours of sleep each night so we can function well during the day. But getting quality sleep isn't merely a chore serving our productivity. Sleep is valuable in its own right and should be prioritized and enjoyed.

__Tricia Hersey__, in her book Rest Is Resistance, *declares that joy and rest are every person's birthright. In her work at __The Nap Ministry__, she creates space for people to nap together in public: a healing, liberatory, and radical experience in direct contrast to capitalist culture's emphasis on productivity.*

Adults spend about one-third of every day sleeping; children need even more sleep as their brains and bodies develop. Without sleep—specifically, without *dreaming* sleep—we can't form new memories. Our brains require this downtime to synthesize and process information, to organize our senses of time and reality. **Exhaustion**—a term we use casually all the time—is, in its formal sense, a medical condition that can lead to health problems and contribute to risky situations. People who aren't getting enough sleep may have trouble remembering things; they may feel nauseous or begin to hallucinate. It's almost as though, if we're deprived of dreams, the dreams will find us one way or another—perhaps while we're awake.

In late 1963 and early 1964, **Randy Gardner**, a teenager from San Diego, California, attempted to break the world record for going the most hours without sleep. Ahead of his school science fair, he got his friends to do everything they could to keep him awake, managing eleven days without a wink. During this time, he suffered from moodiness, heightened sensitivity, paranoia, and decreased cognition. Immediately after breaking the record, Randy was rushed to the hospital for testing; while there, he fell into a deep sleep. The scientists who monitored him concluded that parts of his brain had been catnapping during the experiment, explaining why there wasn't more permanent damage. To discourage others from attempting such a dangerous feat, Guinness World Records has since eliminated the category. In his later years, Gardner complained of chronic insomnia, which he attributed to this experiment in his youth.

THE PHASES OF SLEEP

Sleep is much more complex and eventful than it may seem on the surface. Our brains move through organized cycles of rest and activity throughout the night, and while these rhythms may vary occasionally, our sleeping brains tend to follow a predictable pattern that repeats four to six times, each cycle containing phases of rest and activity.

As we drift off, the first cycle begins with a phase of **light sleep**: Our brains and bodies sink into a state of relaxation. This phase melts into what's known interchangeably as **slow-wave sleep (SWS)**, **non-REM (NREM)**, or **deep sleep**. Our breathing slows and deepens, and our heart rate decelerates; our body temperature cools, our blood pressure decreases, and our muscles slacken. This phase is further broken down into **NREM 1, 2, 3, and 4**: the stages of sleep that are most restorative for the body.

In mammals and birds, the brain then shifts into a state of increased activity—**REM sleep**, the sleep of most dreaming. A section of the brain called the **pons** secretes a chemical that paralyzes the body, preventing it from acting out the scenarios it perceives. Neurons fire rapidly as the brain processes and solves problems. Another name for this phase is **paradoxical sleep**—so-called because although the body is at rest, the mind is active. In fact, the brain tends to consume *more* oxygen and glucose while in paradoxical sleep than it does while awake.

During this time of increased metabolism, the heart rate and breathing speed up again, and we experience **REM (rapid eye movement)**, our eyes darting about beneath our eyelids, tracking invisible stimuli.

*Although most dreaming happens during REM, we sometimes experience short bursts of brain activity during slow-wave sleep, called **sleep spindles**.*

The first phase of REM lasts only about 10 minutes, with each return to REM thereafter lasting longer. Toward the end of a full night's sleep, the dream phase can last 40 minutes or more. Each complete cycle of slow-wave sleep plus REM sleep lasts about 90 to 120 minutes, and as the night goes on, REM dream sleep makes up more of the total, replacing phases 3 and 4 of NREM sleep. This is why we're most likely to remember the dreams that occur closest to waking, as that's the longest period of dreaming we experience. Multiple dreams can take place during each REM phase, and most people experience ten to twenty dream sequences total, adding up to approximately two hours of dreaming each night.

CONSIDER:

While it's important to get enough sleep at night, the quality of our sleep is what's most critical. When we don't get enough deep, restful NREM sleep, we'll be yawning and slow-moving during the day, feeling like all we want to do is curl up under a blanket and go back to bed. On the other hand, when we don't get enough dream-sleep, we might have physical energy, but we'll feel cranky and emotional, like every little thing is a major crisis.

EXPLORE:

To dream, we must sleep, but sleeping doesn't come easily to everyone. Some choices in your waking life can make falling asleep more difficult. You probably already know many of the habits that support good sleep, but it may help to review these tips if you're finding it hard to doze off or to sleep through the night.

* **Cut back on caffeine** (including chocolate, caffeinated sodas, teas, and, most of all, coffee) throughout the day, especially after 2 p.m.
* **Leave two hours between dinner and bedtime,** as your body will spend more of your sleeping energy digesting if you eat right before bed.
* **Get some physical exercise** during the day so your body feels comfortably tired at bedtime.
* **Avoid thinking about stressful things** right before bed.
* **Avoid screens just before bed,** as the blue light activates your brain, telling your body to stay alert.
* **Minimize alcohol and drug use,** since many chemical substances that interact with the brain's chemistry have been shown to shorten REM states.
* **Do your best to allow enough time for sleep.** Seven to nine hours of sleep is often recommended for adults, and if you get less, you're missing out on your last and longest REM cycle—when most of us dream most vividly.

This list may sound nagging, but these factors really do impact your quality of sleep. Throughout this book, you'll find suggestions that promote rest and relaxation. Of course, we can't offer more hours in the day, but you may find that by utilizing your nighttime dream hours to get solid, consistent sleep, the hours you do have become more energized and meaningful.

This week, examine your sleep routine. Is good sleep a priority in your life? If not, how can you adjust your habits to support a healthier balance? Claim your rest and prioritize it as best you can: At least one day this week, go to bed early, sleep in, or indulge in a catnap.

WORKING WITH THE MOON

The moon presides over the dreamworld: a mysterious, silvery counterpart to the golden sun of daytime and waking. Many ancient cultures revered these celestial bodies as partner deities, each with their own qualities, powers, domain, and personality.

For millennia, humans have planned their activities around the moon's phases. A visible, reliable marker of time, the moon informs calendars and the timing of holidays, even now. For example, the Jewish calendar is based on lunar events, as are the Lunar New Year and Harvest Moon festivals celebrated in many Asian cultures. The Christian holiday of Easter is determined by the lunar cycle, falling on the first Sunday after the first full moon on or after the Spring Equinox.

You began your dreamwork journey with the moon as a guide. The instruction to embark under a new moon was, as you may have suspected, not random. The new moon is considered an optimal time to begin new endeavors due to the symbolic significance of starting a cycle anew. The full moon, meanwhile, marks a time of ritual, illumination, and culmination.

CHARTING CYCLES

Each cycle begins with a new moon, and through the next two weeks, it progresses through the waxing crescent and the waxing gibbous phases before revealing its full glory: a round, full moon that bathes our Earth in silver light. Then the moon starts to wane, reversing back through the gibbous and crescent phases until it disappears, beginning the cycle all over again. Through time, people have used the moon's phases to keep track of biological cycles—notably, menstruation. Many believe in the moon's influence over sleep cycles and moods. Hospital workers often anecdotally report upticks in accidents and bizarre behavior under a full moon, and scientific studies suggest that there may indeed be a link.

As you make your way through this book, notice whether you find yourself more attuned to the lunar body. Pay attention to instances when your life aligns with its phases, noting them in your dream journal.

CONSIDER:

Most dreaming happens at night—a time that is often overlooked, taken for granted, or even maligned. Ponder the unique qualities of night, darkness, and shadow. Think about your own relationship to these themes, and spend some time appreciating them for the contrast they bring to our lives.

CONJURE:

Has the moon ever appeared to you in your sleep? See if you can summon it to appear in your dreams this week. Just before bed, spend a few moments gazing up at it in the sky, or look at a picture of it. Ask it to visit you while you sleep.

EXPLORE:

This week, turn your attention to the moon. Notice how it rises and swells, illuminates and goes dark. Appreciate its rhythms. All around the planet, we witness the same moon—a romantic connection between long-distance lovers, a constant companion through turmoil. Countless poems have been written about the moon's mysterious beauty.

Notice how each of these poets assigns a different personality to the moon.

And like a dying lady, lean and pale,
Who totters forth, wrapped in a gauzy veil,
Out of her chamber, led by the insane
And feeble wanderings of her fading brain,
The moon arose up in the murky East,
A white and shapeless mass.

—"The Waning Moon," by Percy Bysshe Shelley

How thin and sharp is the moon tonight!
How thin and sharp and ghostly white
Is the slim curved crook of the moon tonight!

—"Winter Moon," by Langston Hughes

The moon was but a chin of gold
A night or two ago,
And now she turns her perfect face
Upon the world below.

—from "The Moon Was but a Chin of Gold," by Emily Dickinson

WORKING WITH TAROT CARDS

Traditional tarot decks have a card for the Moon and another for the Sun. When a diviner draws the Moon card in a reading, it can represent shadows, secrets, dreams, mystery, reflection, and distortion.

If you have a set of tarot cards, pull the Moon card from your deck and spend some time with it. Carry it with you throughout the week. Notice moments when the card's themes or imagery appear in your daily life. This exercise can help you begin working with symbols, thinking in different ways, and decoding possible meaning. It's also a way to practice keeping things simmering in the back of your mind while you're busy with other tasks.

The Moon card represents emotions and intuition. But it can also have more negative connotations, including deceit and lack of trust—even danger. In tarot, no card is ever inherently good or bad. An individual card's meaning is dependent on its context within a reading.

When you're getting ready for bed, come back to your journal. Write the word "MOON" at the top of a blank page. Jot down any of the reflections or revelations you've had this week, or take some time to free-write about the moon and its qualities.

PLAY:

If it's a clear night, go outside and find the moon. Speak to it; say hello. Blow it a kiss. Make a promise; make a wish. Read it a poem. What personality do *you* see in the moon tonight?

THE SPECTRUM OF CONSCIOUSNESS

Between the poles of consciousness and unconsciousness lies a range of mental states: daydreaming, creativity, imagination, meditation, and more.

Consciousness is realizing you're alive and capable of making intentional decisions about your life. You might feel varying levels of awareness and presence on any given day: Avoidant habits can dull your sense of consciousness, and mindfulness practices can help sharpen it. Anxiety can make you hyperconscious—overly aware of every possible choice.

Unconsciousness is when you are physically alive (heart beating, lungs breathing) but have no awareness of your physical environment. The unconscious mind is the part of your brain that allows you to take action without having to think about it—the "autopilot" mode of operating.

The *subconscious* contains the motivations and impulses that affect your decision-making without your conscious awareness. Examples of subconscious influences are your insecurities, discomforts, biases, attractions, and fears—these things may be rooted in your past, your family, or societal norms and pressures. Often, we might be aware of some of these influences, and when we knowingly factor them into decision-making, we're exercising our conscious mind. But when these things influence us without our acknowledgment, the subconscious is at play.

Altered consciousness generally occurs when there's a change in brain function, leading a person to experience reality differently than usual. Consciousness can be altered through the consumption of drugs or alcohol or through physical changes to the brain, such as a tumor, injury, aneurysm, or mental illness. Altered consciousness can also be pursued through practices like meditation, sleep deprivation, or fasting, or it can come about through sudden, intense changes like shock, grief, or stress. During periods of altered consciousness, people sometimes hallucinate—seeing, hearing, or feeling things that don't exist in physical reality.

Transcendence is defined by a sense of profoundness or unity that often leaves one with a new awareness of the interconnectedness of all beings. These experiences are often ineffable—beyond words. For some, transcendent experiences are overwhelming and might be avoided or repressed. For others, transcendence is a deeply desirable state worth pursuing, perhaps over the course of a lifetime. Enlightened beings, such as Buddhist monks, saints, and other religious figures, allegedly exist in longer (even permanent) states of transcendent consciousness.

PLAY:

By engaging in dreamwork, you can grow more comfortable with your inner voice and deepen trust in your intuition. Dreaming is an opportunity to be in conversation with yourself and the universe.

This week, conduct a **self-interview**—a dialogue with your dream-self. Play with the idea that this is an aspect of yourself that has adventures each night while your body rests. You can write down your questions and answers in your journal, or talk out loud to yourself.

Ask your dream-self about the realm they inhabit. You might ask about a specific dream that's been puzzling you, or you may want to keep the conversation more general, asking whether your dream-self has any messages for you. Close your eyes and be still as you wait for a response—the reply could come in words, images, or some other kind of understanding.

EXPLORE:

In the midst of your daily routines and responsibilities this week, pause occasionally. Try setting a few random alarms throughout the day, and when they go off, make a mental note of where your brain is on the spectrum of consciousness at that moment. Are you acting out of habit? Daydreaming? In active concentration? Whatever your state of mind, take a moment to bring a deeper awareness to your actions. Pay attention to your senses—what you see around you, what you smell and feel—and take a few deep breaths. Try to extend these moments of mindfulness.

CHECK IN:

At the close of your first month of dreamwork, take a moment to acknowledge this accomplishment and reflect on what the experience was like for you. Ponder these questions in your dream journal:

HOW'S IT GOING?

* How has it felt to record your dreams this past month?
* Have you been recording as often as you'd like and in a way that works for you?

WHAT'S CHANGED?

* Have you noticed any differences in your dreaming so far?
* How about changes in your waking life?

ARE YOU READY TO MOVE FORWARD?

* Is it time to move on to the next cycle? If so, take a moment to recommit to your dreams. Will you move ahead with the same intention as last month, or is there something else you'd like to focus on?

DREAMING JOURNEY:
PREHISTORY

Cave walls all over the world are adorned with strange, zoomorphic figures: humans with antlers, an animal head on a human body—not the stuff of ordinary life but images of spiritual significance to the people who painted them. Archaeologists suggest that many of these cave paintings were inspired by dreams and that people used whatever media they had on hand—charcoal or mud paint—to record their mysterious, fleeting visions.

The brains of ancient humans were anatomically very similar to our own and likely operated in much the same way. For this reason, we can assume that most prehistoric dreams, like modern ones, were populated by the people, tasks, and objects of day-to-day life. For a prehistoric person, this would have meant basic survival: hunting and gathering, seeking shelter, and honing tools from stone. Our Paleolithic ancestors might have dreamed about picking weeds or finding good rocks to flintknap. Perhaps they dreamt of seeing an attractive face flickering in the firelight, or, occasionally, of fleeing a saber-toothed tiger.

More rarely, they may have experienced an exceptional dream: a prophetic dream or a dream of guidance, so vivid and strange that it seemed to come from a place beyond the dreamer's own mind—perhaps from another realm entirely. Nowadays, such dreams are commonly dismissed; they might be shared with friends after a few drinks or become the subject of an online post, if not forgotten. But in prehistoric times, these kinds of dreams were almost certainly revered, understood as having come from a powerful, external place or force. They may also have been deliberately summoned through the transcendent power of ritual and trance.

Caves have long been understood as portals to the beyond. Often, the strangest paintings are found in caves that are difficult to access, indicating they were sought out for their sacred qualities. While we can't know what took place within those dark passages, historians theorize they were host to rituals meant to trigger epiphanies or feelings of lucidity. The paintings left there may record the visions our ancestors conjured—or they may be evidence of the conjuring itself.

PREHISTORY is generally defined as the time before humans wrote things down—but writing isn't the only kind of record, so even without written documents, anthropologists can still speculate about the lives of our human ancestors who existed hundreds of thousands of years ago.

CYCLE II

WARMING UP

CYCLE II WEEK 1 NEW MOON

DEEP RELAXATION

Relaxation is not only an important benefit of sleep and dreaming; it is also crucial to falling asleep in the first place. If you have trouble getting to sleep, you may want to spend some time consciously welcoming relaxation to your body. Even if sleep comes easily to you, focusing on relaxation can help you reach a deeper state of rest.

EXPLORE:

Breathing is a fundamental way to calm the body and bring awareness to the present moment. Over the next week, spend a couple of minutes each evening focusing on your breath in an effort to relax your body and mind. Try this simple exercise before bed:

* Lie flat on your back with your legs out before you. Put your right hand over your heart and your left hand on your belly.
* Breathe in deeply, taking it slow—feel your belly rise first, then your chest. Hold the breath in your lungs for a slow count of three. Then slowly breathe out, deflating your chest and then belly.
* Repeat this, allowing each exhale to match the length of your inhale. After a few cycles, see if you can make the exhale longer than your inhale.

Imagine you are releasing the stresses of your day with each exhale: Let go of stagnation, frustration, blocks, and anything else you wish to relinquish before you enter the dreamworld.

Yoga Nidra, *or yogic sleep, translates to "peace beyond words" or "blissful relaxation" and is first mentioned in the Indian epic Mahabharata. Today, this term refers to a restorative practice that integrates older yogic traditions with relaxation techniques to help people slip into a state of deep bodily relaxation. Using breath as a rhythmic guide, a practitioner slowly and systematically directs their energy to specific muscle sets, tensing and then releasing them. You might begin with the muscles in the face, then move down the neck and across the shoulders, following the lines of the arms to the fingers; down the torso, the curve of the back, and the genitals; down the thighs, calves, and feet. By focusing on your body and breath, your mind becomes calm and relaxed, and sleep becomes more easily accessible.*

PLAY:

We breathe constantly and automatically to stay alive. Bring some attention to the different phases within this simple, essential cycle.

INHALE

* **Take the outside in:** Eat, smell, watch, listen, taste, feel.

HOLD

* **Process what is received:** Make value judgments (That smells *bad*! That movie was *fun*!), form hypotheses, and draw conclusions based on what you've taken in and your relationship to it.

EXHALE

* **How do you let the inside out?** How do you share your conclusions and opinions? How do you impact your environment?

REFLECT:

Continue to record your dreams. Notice whether this week's focus on breathing and relaxation has any effect on your sleep.

One or two nights this week, take some time to **transcribe your dreams**. Type them in a word processor or copy them by hand in neater or more elaborate handwriting. What effect does this action have on your connection to these entries? If you feel like embellishing your entries with new details you remember or invent, go for it. Alter, amend, play!

Remember: Dream truths, more than those of waking life, are fluid.

CONSIDER:

Cycles and circulation, giving and receiving, ebbs and flows, the invisible and the essential. Think about the relationship of air and your breath to dreaming; perhaps you want to journal about these ideas or sketch something with them in mind.

CYCLE II WEEK 2 WAXING MOON

MAPPING YOUR WAKING LIFE

There are countless theories about why we dream, where dreams come from, and what they mean—some are described on page 69. Dreams can be universal, connecting the dreamer to something greater than their individual self; they can also be highly subjective and personal. Dreams show us that conflicting or paradoxical truths can coexist.

One of the most common modern-day theories of dreaming is that dreams are a tool our brains use to process the events—particularly the stresses—of daily life. They are filled with what Sigmund Freud called **day residues**: elements of our waking lives that resurface in the subconscious. We can sift through these dreams to determine what we might really feel, to gain insight, or to work through something that hasn't been fully resolved.

To work with these kinds of dreams, it can be helpful to map out the major domains of your daily life. You can then refer back to this map and use it to decode your dreams.

PLAY:

Try taking the "map" prompt literally and think about how to spatially arrange your list, perhaps as a web or network of connecting points. You may find that different areas branch off from each other like landforms; others might exist as islands. Later, after you dream, try tracing a course through this landscape, allowing the dream's elements—its themes, narrative, and characters—to guide your way.

CONJURE:

In the first week of dreamwork, we explored working with intentions. This week, practice honing your intention further, tailoring it to suit a nightly goal. For example, you might aim to be shown a map of your life.

Ground yourself with a deep breath. Speak aloud or write in your journal: "I will see a map of my life tonight." You could also phrase your intention as a humble request: "Dreams, please show me the landscape of my life tonight."

When you wake to write in your journal this week, focus on describing where you were in your dream. What was the terrain or environment like? What answers did your dream offer—how might your dream's setting reflect where you are in life right now? Assume that whatever you were shown was relevant in some way to your request.

CONSIDER:

Dreams and emotions are like two flowers along the same stem: Both can arise from external stimuli, and both can signal deeper work happening in the subconscious. Dreams often have emotional undertones, so following them to their root can help untangle your feelings about something you may not have come to terms with. In turn, this allows you to address underlying issues to eventually encourage new growth.

EXPLORE:

This week, examine your life and write down a few keywords for each of the categories and prompts listed below. Pay particular attention to any stresses or unresolved areas. It's likely that your responses will change or develop over the course of your dreamwork, so feel free to return to this map and update it as needed.

Use objective language, stating just the facts without emotion or judgment. These situations can have weighty feelings attached, but this isn't the place to explore them. Keep it simple.

Skip any categories that don't apply, and feel free to add topics or issues that are particular to your life.

HINT: *Human life is messy! The idea here is not to compartmentalize your life into neat little boxes but rather to sketch out its landscape. Use broad strokes to give a basic impression of where you are right now.*

PERSONAL TERRAINS

RELATIONSHIPS: Which romantic relationships, professional partnerships, friendships, or family bonds are at the center of your life right now?

CREATIVITY: What hobbies, crafts, or other creative pursuits matter to you right now?

HEALTH: How is your physical and mental health? Have you experienced any recent changes in your well-being?

FINANCES: Is this a time of material abundance for you, or are you feeling a sense of struggle or scarcity?

SPIRITUALITY: How would you describe your spiritual state?

HOME: What's happening in your living environment? Are there any tensions or stressors in your household?

SOCIETY: What larger political or cultural issues are on your mind?

ART AND CULTURE: What books, music, or other media have moved or affected you lately?

OTHER: Here, you may want to note any trauma or unresolved issues from your past, such as grief, addiction, injury, abuse, childhood issues, systemic pressure, etc. These things may or may not be on your mind daily, but they can easily rear up in dreams. Make note of them and be aware of their potential influence.

CYCLE II WEEK 3 FULL MOON

STRENGTHENING DREAM RECALL

Studies have shown that within five minutes of waking, we forget 50 percent of what we dream, and by the time ten minutes have passed, 90 percent of our dream has dissolved back into the ether. In general, when you're not actively dedicating time to remembering and writing down your dreams, only a very intense, vivid dream will stay with you. A dream's natural tendency is to vanish. But if we believe that dreams are useful, it helps to be able to remember them.

CONSIDER:

One of the most magical things about dreams is that they work for you without your active direction. If you're sleeping, you're dreaming, and if you're dreaming, you're processing your waking life. As you give more care to your dreams, you'll become more familiar with how this process unfolds for you personally.

EXPLORE:

Some simple tools and techniques can assist with dream recall. This week, try out one or more of these strategies.

* **Set an alarm.** If you use an alarm to wake up in the morning, make a habit of setting it five to ten minutes earlier than you need to. Set it to a calm sound, since loud disruption can agitate your body into a state of urgency, causing all memory of your dreams to slip away. You want to remain as relaxed as possible upon waking to encourage your dreams to stay with you.
* **Keep still.** Ease into action, prolonging the liminal state between dreaming and waking. Try not to move when you first wake up, as movement will activate your neurons and muscles, disturbing that embodied sense of peace.
* **Give your dream a name.** To name a thing is to form a relationship with it. A name can sum up what something is all about or imbue it with a sense of intrigue. Return to your dream journal and title some of your dreams as though they were television episodes, short stories, or songs.
* **Try ginkgo biloba.** The fruit of the ginkgo tree is said to support healthy brain function, specifically aiding in memory retrieval. If your doctor confirms this herb is safe for you, you can find it in supplements, tinctures, teas, or fruits at many health food stores and Asian markets.

* **Carry your dream journal with you throughout the day.** This way, if you happen to remember something from a dream, you can jot it down immediately. Treating your journal as a valuable, essential tool also reaffirms the significance of your dreamwork. Just remember to place it under your pillow or on your nightstand again at night.

CHECK IN:

You've made a commitment to dreamwork, and hopefully, you're starting to see some results. Over the past few weeks, you've begun remembering your dreams with a little more clarity and frequency, and you've been making time to record them.

Read through what you've written in your journal so far. Do memories of your past dreams return to you easily, or do they feel utterly foreign now? Does anything stand out?

PLAY:

Turn to the illustration on page 99. Set a timer and stare at it for thirty seconds, soaking up as many details as you can. Afterward, without referring back to the image, see if you can answer these questions about it:

* What animals were in the illustration?
* How many insects did you find?
* What types of plant life did you see?
* Where were the birds in the illustration, and what were they doing?

Throughout this week, periodically practice this skill. Look out the window for a solid minute, then turn away and try to remember what you saw and heard in detail. When you're on the bus or train, or in some other public place, observe your surroundings. Later, test yourself: *How many people were sitting across from me? What color was the man's jacket?* Developing your observational skills in waking life can help you notice and remember more in your dreams, too.

CYCLE II WEEK 4 WANING MOON

THE STUFF OF DREAMS

The things we do frequently, the things we often think, what we see regularly—these are likely to appear in our dreams. Often, our dreams are rife with things we might consider boring or unimportant. But it's possible to use our dreams as an early diagnostic tool, noticing what concerns us and what we prioritize, so we can resolve and redirect our thoughts if we want to.

Thoughts don't have body or shape; we make them tangible when we put them into words, either by writing them down or sharing them verbally. Externalizing thoughts—giving them form through language—is powerful magic.

NEUROPLASTICITY

Who we are—what we think and do—is not set in stone. The mind is a flexible mechanism; like a muscle, it retains elasticity with exercise. Neurons are looking to connect, and the things we do regularly cause synapses to fire, creating neural pathways that become familiar. We figure out what works for us and tend to call on the same skills and shortcuts repeatedly, eventually cementing neural pathways into habits. As we age, some patterns and habits can begin to feel like they limit or stunt us; depression and trauma can decrease the number of synapses in our brains, also making it harder to stay flexible. However, as long as we're alive, our brains possess **neuroplasticity**, the ability to change and adapt—even if it requires a little more effort as we get older.

SUPPORTING NEUROPLASTICITY

Daily physical exercise—even just a nice, long walk—increases neuroplasticity. It helps the brain stay fit and active as much as it benefits the rest of the body. You can also strengthen your neural health by getting good sleep, trying things outside your comfort zone, being social, making art, traveling, learning new skills (how to play a new instrument or speak a foreign language), and . . . by spending time with your dreams. In fact, the **defensive activation theory** proposes that we dream to keep our visual neurons busy while we sleep, strengthening neuroplasticity!

Dreams alone won't necessarily solve deep psychological issues, but they can be used in conjunction with other supports to improve outcomes. Our dreams can help redirect us toward healthier habits, healing, and growth.

REFLECT:

What habits do you have? We're not here to judge whether a habit is good or bad, useful or harmful. Just think about habits as things you do repeatedly, perhaps without thinking. Going deeper, ask yourself what purpose your habits serve—what do they do or provide for you?

If some of your habits distract you or take from you more than they give, ask yourself if you might turn your energy and attention in a healthier direction.

EXPLORE:

Dreams can help you become more aware of habits that cause you trouble. Try setting a nightly intention to explore your habits, formulating it as a statement or a request. Here are a few examples:

- I wish to be shown where this habit originated.
- I am seeking healthier ways to cope with the stresses of life.
- Please help me face my temptation toward this habit.
- Tonight, show me my habit embodied in a physical form—perhaps as a person or creature.

CONSIDER:

Habits can be a way to self-medicate or patch over wounds: a survival tactic. Breaking a habit without addressing why you needed it in the first place could lead you to pick up another unhealthy habit in its place.

Ask yourself about the deeper issue: Does this habit offer comfort? Escape? Does it guard against boredom? Trauma? Insecurity?

PLAY:

Identify a harmless habit in your waking life and try redirecting it to see what new information you can glean. For example, if you walk the same route to work every day, try taking a different path. Try tea instead of coffee in the morning; shake up your work or lunchtime routine. See what it feels like to do things with your nondominant hand for a day: brushing your teeth, writing notes, opening doors, etc.

Does this practice open you up to new ways of thinking? Does it have any effect on your dreams this week?

DREAMING JOURNEY:
MESOPOTAMIA

Our very oldest texts contain records of dreams. The earliest known written language is **cuneiform**, found etched into clay cylinders and tablets from the ancient Mesopotamian empire of the Fertile Crescent—modern-day Iran and Iraq. These artifacts date back more than four thousand years, and while they mostly document bureaucratic matters, the ancient Stele of Vultures monument also describes a visitation by a god to a sleeping king, ensuring his success in battle. Other tablets from this region depict consultations with **Nanshe**, the ancient Mesopotamian goddess of prophecy, and the messages she sent through dreams in reply. From these artifacts, we know dreaming served a number of purposes for the Mesopotamians—primarily those of guidance and future telling.

ASSYRIAN DREAM BOOKS

Some of the oldest artifacts in existence are the **Assyrian Dream Books**, a collection of clay tablets found in the library of King Ashurbanipal at Nineveh, near modern-day Mosul, Iraq. These tablets not only record significant dreams but also list their interpretations and noted omens.

If he carries beer in the street, his heart will be glad.
If he carries water in the street, his sins will be forgiven.
If he lolls his tongue, goodness of heart will not be granted him.

To address those dreams we don't wish to remember, the tablets describe a ritual called "bur," in which the dreamer recounts their bad dream to a lump of mud, drops the lump into water, and recites this incantation to dissolve it:

Like a clod thrown in water, may the dream be destroyed in its trickling!

Other Mesopotamian dream records from this period contain puns—for example, dreaming of a raven (*arbu*) meant you would make some money (*irbu*) in the near future. Wordplay is a common feature in dream reports from around the world, even today.

GILGAMESH

One of humanity's oldest preserved epics is the story of the demigod Mesopotamian king GILGAMESH. Believed to date back to over four thousand years ago, this tale was passed down orally for centuries before it was recorded. It serves as a window into how people of the time understood the nature of dreams—specifically, the special connection between dreams and the gods. Gods could direct and influence mortal decisions through dreams, could give warnings, and could even predict events. Kings were believed to descend from the gods, and they often used dreamwork to confirm their power and authority.

In this epic, Gilgamesh is a tyrant who abuses his power, so the gods intervene. They create **Enkidu**: a new, wilder version of Gilgamesh who is half-human, half-animal—a very dreamlike amalgamation—to restore peace and balance to the kingdom of Uruk.

Unaware of this, Gilgamesh has a series of dreams that he brings to his mother to "untie" or interpret. In Mesopotamia, dream interpreters were usually women gifted at analyzing symbols and metaphors. First, Gilgamesh tells his mother that he dreamed a shooting star fell on him from the skies—a star he could neither lift nor move. Next, he tells her about a dream during which an axe fell from the sky and hugged him like a wife.

Gilgamesh's mother explains that these dreams represent a companion entering his life. That companion turns out to be Enkidu, who enters the city of Uruk, fights Gilgamesh, then becomes his good friend when they realize they are equally matched, like two sides of the same coin. Together, Enkidu and Gilgamesh join forces to fight a bigger threat: the monster **Humbaba**. Gilgamesh grows as a person through his journeys with Enkidu, and again through grief when his friend dies.

Note the nature of these dreams: highly symbolic, rich, mysterious, and poetic. Gilgamesh knew immediately upon waking that these were prophetic dreams—dreams that relayed valuable information about his circumstances and his future. He knew that if he could untangle the language of symbols, he would better direct and control his fortune. Ultimately, his dreams transformed him by leading him to see beyond his ego and thirst for power.

CYCLE III

THE SENSES

CYCLE III WEEK 1 ○ NEW MOON

SENSORY PROCESSING

Our experience of the waking world is determined, in large part, by information we gather from our senses. Typically, when we talk about our senses, we mean the big five: sight, hearing, touch, smell, and taste. Not everyone has access to all these senses, and we all experience them with varying degrees of sensitivity. Furthermore, there exist many senses beyond these five—emotional, barometric, proprioceptive, spatial, etc.

In our waking life, when we see or hear things that others don't—and there's no physical cause—it's called a hallucination and often considered cause for alarm. In dreams, our senses aren't collecting concrete, physical data, yet we experience our dreams as if they were real, all the same.

EXPLORE:

This week, explore how your senses shape your experience of daily life. Take a series of **sensory walks** around your neighborhood, each one focused on a different sense. On the first walk, focus on sight: Notice what catches your eye up close and far away, from the smallest details to the broadest views. On the next walk, bring awareness to sound: the layers of noise around you, both subtle and pronounced. If you wish to continue, dedicate your next walk to touch: Observe the sensation of your feet against the ground, the temperature of the air on your skin, and your overall sense of physical comfort (or discomfort).

Take particular note of the smells, sounds, images, and feelings that uplift your mood. These small pleasures can become tools in shaping a more restful sleep routine. Notice what brings you calm, joy, or a sense of ease—and make space for more of it.

PLAY:

For those who can access it, sight is often the most dominant sense—both in waking life and in dreams. In fact, in many languages, instead of "having" a dream, people say they "see" a dream.

Still, our other senses contribute valuable information, even if their influence is less immediate.

To become more aware of these senses, try closing your eyes when you listen, taste, touch, or smell.

Synesthesia is a blending of two or more senses, in which things might "sound blue" or "taste velvety," for example. Have you ever experienced this in your dreams? How about in waking life? Pay attention to these overlaps, or experiment with creating your own. For instance, try doodling to music and see what shapes or colors your mind associates with different sounds.

CHECK IN:

Review your dreams again—this time, with a pen in hand. Make a mark next to things that stand out upon rereading: evocative imagery, interesting phrases, or things you might want to investigate further. Note instances when something from your dreams later appears in waking life. Jot down any new insights into what your dreams may have meant. Sometimes our dreams become easier to interpret after some time has passed.

Carry on recording at least one dream a week.

EARLY SLEEP STUDIES

In the 1950s, when graduate student **Eugene Aserinsky** was assigned to the University of Chicago's sleep lab, he wasn't thrilled. Like most scientists at the time, he believed that sleep was little more than a passive state in which the brain and body shut down.

But as his research progressed, Aserinsky grew more curious. He began to suspect that the twitching of a sleeper's eyes might correlate to increased brain activity—to dreaming. To investigate, he brought his eight-year-old son to the lab and hooked him up to a primitive electroencephalogram (EEG) machine that graphed his brain waves. As his son drifted into early sleep, the EEG showed slow, steady waves, but hours later, Aserinsky noticed the pens on the machine suddenly jerking in sharp, erratic patterns—usually a sign of wakefulness or machine error. When he checked, his son was still fast asleep, though his eyes were darting beneath his eyelids. This was "rapid eye movement," or REM—a phase when the eyes follow the images seen in dreams.

REM had been observed before, but Aserinsky's use of the EEG provided the first clear link between REM and increased brain activity. Through further experimentation, he showed that sleep unfolds in repeating cycles, and that in some parts of these cycles, the brain is as active as it is during wakefulness. He also showed that everyone dreams, even if they don't remember it.

CYCLE III WEEK 2 WAXING MOON

DREAMS AND SOUND

DREAMING LEADS TO MUSIC . . .

Sound, especially music, can be used to influence sleep and dreams—and in turn, dreams have inspired music throughout history. One famous example is the classic Beatles song "Yesterday," which came to Paul McCartney fully formed in a dream. Likewise, Igor Stravinsky's *The Rite of Spring*—the story of a girl who dances herself to death in a pagan ritual—came to him in a dream while he was working on *The Firebird* during the day. It was such a departure from the music of the time that it caused controversy: The audience was upset, suspecting Stravinsky was mocking them with the music's unpredictable rhythms and jarring loudness. Nowadays, however, *The Rite of Spring* is considered one of the foundational works of modernism. Art inspired by dreams often has this dual quality: It is at once unique and innovative, yet timeless and classic.

RAHSAAN ROLAND KIRK AND THE RELIGION OF DREAMS

Rahsaan Roland Kirk was a jazz genius—or, as he described himself, a Black classical musician devoted to the "religion of dreams." He skillfully played just about any instrument he picked up, including ones he invented himself. Kirk was renowned for his unique performances, often appearing onstage with multiple horns around his neck, harmonizing with himself by playing different instruments simultaneously. He explained that he was bringing forth the dream-inspired music he constantly heard in his head.

Blinded at birth when a nurse put too much silver nitrate in his eyes, Kirk relied on dreams to guide him through his life and musical career. Perhaps this is why he pushed the boundaries of music—crafting instruments from things such as garden hoses, alarm clocks, and more, using his innovative sounds to disrupt the injustices of the status quo.

Combining his passions for music and civil rights, Kirk formed **The Jazz and People's Movement**, an organization of musicians who protested cultural institutions that overlooked Black artists while lauding and financially rewarding the white musicians who were inspired by them.

. . . AND MUSIC LEADS TO DREAMING

Lullabies, like dreams, are found in most cultures. Despite the tenderness inherent in a song designed to soothe a baby to sleep, many of these tunes contain strange, frightening lyrics or haunting melodies: "Rock-a-Bye Baby" ends with the cradle falling from the tree, baby and all; and the Russian song "Bayu Bayushki Bayu" warns children not to sleep too close to the edge of the bed, lest a wolf come to drag them into the woods. This blending of fear and comfort is reminiscent of the dreamworld itself. It can also reflect the sometimes-desperate state of new parents stuck in a perpetual twilight, trying to get their baby to fall asleep.

PLAY:

Both music and dreams can connect us to the past—our own past, or further back, the experiences of our ancestors. Do you have any memories of songs from when you were a baby or small child? Perhaps you can ask your family if there were any melodies they sang to you, or ones their parents sang to them. If you don't have this kind of memory or relationship, perhaps you can look up lullabies or folk songs from your ancestral culture(s).

This week, connect with your own voice and *SING*. Even if you've been told you have a bad voice or are tone deaf, belt out a song you love in the privacy of your own home—or while you're out walking. Connecting with your voice can be a powerful affirmation of self.

DREAM DIRECTOR

Conceptual artist **Luke Jerram** designed an installation called **The Dream Director,** in which participants spent the night inside individual pods in a large gallery space. Bridging art and science, Jerram attempted to "sculpt" others' dreams using sound, his goal to create artwork inside the slumbering mind.

Readying themselves for sleep, participants donned masks that monitored eye movement, and once REM was detected, Jerram pumped soundscapes into their pods. Upon waking, many attendees reported pleasant dreams, noting the influence of sounds matching those Jerram had played while they slept.

REFLECT:

Sound can do more than just soothe a person to sleep. Scientists and artists alike have experimented with the effects sound can have on dreams, and vice versa. Have you ever had an experience in which a sound in the waking world—a phone alarm or an ambulance siren—entered your consciousness while you slept? It's a common trope in movies.

EXPLORE:

Before bed, experiment with sound, seeing how it influences your sleep and dreams.

* First, decide what kind of mood you want to create within your dreams, then choose recordings that foster that kind of atmosphere. Press "Play," and listen until you drift off to sleep. Try different styles of music throughout the week to see how each affects the quality and content of your dreams.

HINT: *If sleep is a struggle for you, you may want to stick to calm, quiet songs or instrumental pieces. You can also reach beyond formal compositions and try out soothing soundscapes from nature and elsewhere.*

* After you record your dreams in the morning, note the influence of these different soundtracks.

A SAMPLE SEVEN-NIGHT AUDITORY SCHEDULE

NIGHT 1: Ambient soundscapes, e.g., ocean waves, crickets in a cornfield, rain on a city street

NIGHT 2: Repetitive sounds, such as chanting, drumming, or droning

NIGHT 3: Lullabies

NIGHT 4: Ethereal instrumental or choral music

NIGHT 5: Binaural tones

Binaural tones (or binaural beats) *are an auditory illusion: When you wear stereo headphones and play a different tone in each ear, your brain creates a third tone between the two frequencies. Binaural tones are said to influence brain activity, inducing states of deep calm or focus. While you won't get the full effect without headphones, ambient recordings can be soothing on their own, and they can be found in many places online.*

NIGHT 6: A playlist of songs with the word "dream" in the lyrics

NIGHT 7: Music from your ancestral culture(s)

CYCLE III WEEK 3 FULL MOON

SMELL AND TASTE

Smell has a powerful connection to memory because the brain's olfactory center is located near the area responsible for storing past experiences. Certain smells—a familiar perfume, fresh-baked goodies, woodsmoke—might conjure vivid memories. A dear one's scent on a piece of clothing can make it feel as though they are right there with you. Other times, particular smells can create a vague sense of nostalgia, much like dreams, evoking strong feelings while remaining just out of reach.

Taste can also enhance your dreamwork. One traditional way to include the taste buds is to drink tea made from herbs associated with dreaming. Most grocery stores offer some sort of dream- or sleep-themed tea, while herbalists and other health practitioners can provide more specific recommendations. If you have a green thumb, you can deepen your relationship with tea by growing your own plants, drying their leaves, and filling reusable tea bags with them.

Alternatively, many dream-promoting herbs are available as **tinctures** in health food stores, offering a more concentrated version of their properties. Add a dropperful of tincture to a glass of water and drink it before bed, paying special attention to its taste.

HINT: *Be sure to consult with a medical professional before consuming herbal teas or tinctures, as these can sometimes interact with medications or exacerbate existing health conditions. It's also important to note the distinction between a tincture and an essential oil; essential oils are for smelling, not tasting.*

EXPLORE:

Lavender and **chamomile** are well-known for their soothing properties, produced by the chemical oils in their leaves and flowers. **Mugwort** is a powerful dream herb, tending to grow wild in liminal spaces, along train tracks or by the edges of highways. It has long been linked to the dreamworld in folklore and herbal medicine. In fact, in the Middle Ages, when witchcraft was outlawed as heresy, herbalists in Europe would plant mugwort outside their homes as a secret indicator of who lived there.

Other herbs that are said to support your dreamwork include:

* **Rosemary:** Enhances memory and dream recall
* **Tulsi (holy basil):** Promotes relaxation and a sense of well-being
* **Lemon balm:** Offers gentle calming
* **Rose petals:** Adds a touch of sensuality
* **Peppermint:** Enhances lucid dreaming and vivid dreams
* **Passionflower:** Acts as a sedative
* **Anise/licorice:** Encourages more pleasant dreams and keeps nightmares away

You can crush the leaves or petals of these plants to release their fragrance, or experiment with them in other forms, like incense, essential oils, or sprays.

PLAY:

Once you've settled on the specific scents you're drawn to, incorporate them into your sleep ritual by concocting a **dream oil**. Since smell is so strongly linked to memory, over time you'll begin to associate your signature dream scent with sleep.

Select two or three essential oils with fragrances that appeal to you. Add a few drops of each to a mostly full two-ounce bottle of carrier oil, such as coconut or almond oil. Shake to blend, and store in a cool, dark place.

WAYS TO USE YOUR DREAM OIL:

* Anoint your temples and inner wrists with a little oil before sleep.

HINT: *Some essential oils can be irritating to the skin. Research the oils you use and be sure they're safe for topical application.*

* Enhance your written dream intention by placing a drop of dream oil on your finger and drawing it across your words. Tuck the scented paper under your pillow, or roll it up and store it near your heart—in the breast pocket of your pajamas or a locket.
* Add a splash of your dream oil to a small spray bottle, diluting it with witch hazel (available at most pharmacies) in a 1:1 ratio. Shake it up and spritz your pillow and sleep area to clear and scent the atmosphere.

HINT: *You can also use your spray to energetically cleanse your dream journal if you've been carrying it around with you during the day.*

* Dress an unscented candle with dream oil, using your fingertips to rub a little oil onto the wax, thinking about your dream intention while you do so.

REFLECT:

Have you ever smelled or tasted something in your dreams? Sight and hearing are the most common senses experienced in dreams, but occasionally we might access other senses. If you experience taste or smell while dreaming, be sure to note it in your journal.

CYCLE III WEEK 4  WANING MOON

DREAMS AND TOUCH

When we're asleep, we're less aware of the body. Indeed, in some cultures it's believed that the soul leaves the body during sleep to go on its own adventures.

Touch, more than any other sense, is wedded to the material world. To be touched, a thing must have substance and form. Even still, we can sometimes experience physical sensations in the dreaming realm. When we feel touch in a dream—a space of immateriality–it can be truly bewildering.

A **lidérc** is a Hungarian demon believed to hatch from a black hen's egg warmed in manure. It attaches itself to a human host, often targeting unhappy lovers, and sucks their blood at night while feeding them erotic dreams, leaving them restless, weak, and ill. The trade-off is that the lidérc also hoards gold and can make its host rich. So, what'll it be? Keep the lidérc and become wealthy, or kick it out and get your sleep back? To get rid of the lidérc, you must trick it into attempting an impossible task–like collecting water in a sieve–then lock it inside a hollow tree.

Sometimes the sensations we experience in our dreams can prompt real, physical responses in the body. For example, the relaxed state of sleep can stimulate blood flow to the genitals, which can lead to erections and even orgasm, especially in early adolescence. In medieval times, Christian monks thought such experiences were demonic in nature—the results of an evil curse or temptations sent by the devil. Today we know that erotic, sexually stimulating dreams are natural, and most people experience them at some point in their lives. Instead of casting judgment on a dream like this, explore what it might tell you about yourself, your desires, or your subconscious. You can also simply enjoy it for what it is.

Another somewhat common tactile dream is the **fight dream**, in which the dreamer engages in a physical altercation of some kind. This might be a way for the subconscious to safely release pent-up stress, frustration, or aggression, though a fight dream that doesn't end in victory may also reveal feelings of impotence or powerlessness.

The lidérc can appear as a featherless chicken or as a ball of light.

PLAY:

To relax your body and bring extra attention to physical sensations, treat yourself to a **dream bath**.

* **Choose a sleep outfit:** Before your bath, lay out your favorite pajamas or a large cotton T-shirt. Special sleepwear adds an air of significance to the ritual.
* **Prepare the bath:** As you fill the tub, add herbs or flower petals and a few drops of your dream oil to the water. Alternatively, you may want to try bubbles or bath salts. Light candles around the tub, dim or turn off the lights, and put on some soothing music.
* **Relax:** Slow your breathing as you settle into the water. Draw attention to the physical sensations within and around your body. Inhale the calming scents and let your mind drift along to the music, luxuriating in the warmth of the bath.

HINT: *If you don't have a bathtub, adapt this ritual to the shower or fill a large bowl with warm water for a foot bath.*

When you're ready, pull the plug and visualize your stresses swirling down the drain with the water. Dry yourself off with a soft towel and step into your sleep outfit.

MORE TIPS FOR ENHANCING YOUR SENSE OF TOUCH BEFORE BED:

* **Moisturize:** Apply a moisturizer or cream to your arms and legs, gently massaging your body as you do so.
* **Keep cool:** Ensure your sleep space is kept cool through the night, ideally below 70 degrees Fahrenheit.
* **Stretch your body:** Lie in child's pose for a few breaths (page 133), or do a few slow neck and shoulder rolls before you fall asleep.

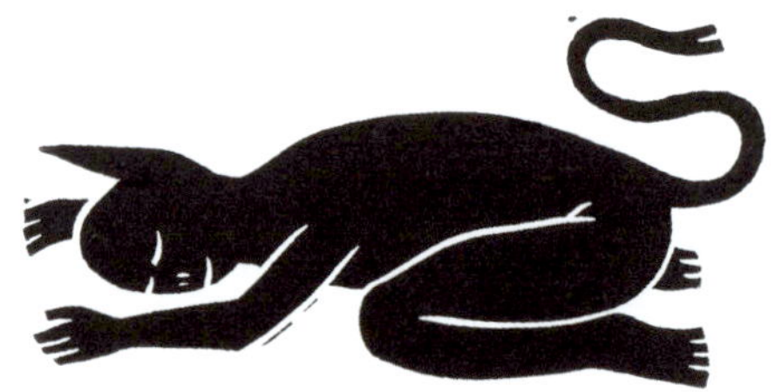

EXPLORE:

This week, bring more awareness to your body. Pay close attention to the sensations at your fingertips and nerve endings. Notice the feel of your fingers on the keyboard as you type, the touch of a fork on your tongue, or a breeze on your skin. Observe things closely but without judgment: the lines on your palm, your shoelaces, the pattern or weave of your shirt's fabric. This increased attention to detail might carry into your dreams.

CONJURE:

Before sleep, consciously invite other senses into your dreams. Using the intention-setting techniques discussed in the first week of dreamwork, try writing or speaking one of the following statements to encourage a fuller sensory experience in your dreams:

I will taste something in
my dreams tonight.

*

I am open to feeling sensation
in my dreams tonight.

*

I welcome a full sensory
experience to my dreams.

However, as you may have already noticed, dreams don't always respond to direct requests or commands. Experiment with different ways of invoking an intention this week: Maybe you'll have more success idly meditating on the idea of "taste" before sleep, for example, or you might casually jot down your intention at midday, then do your best to forget about it.

CONSIDER:

Sometimes our dreams speak to us without words, symbols, or metaphors. You might simply wake up with a ringing insight: clear knowledge of what you should do or avoid. This kind of clairsentience, *or knowledge beyond perception, is a gift from dreams, whether it comes from deep within or from a power beyond. Make sure you write down or otherwise record the information you received so it doesn't slip away.*

REFLECT:

Have you ever felt physical pain or pleasure in a dream? Try to recall the circumstances and consider what insight you might've gained from the experience.

DREAMING JOURNEY:

CLASSICAL ANTIQUITY

ANCIENT EGYPT

Ancient Egyptians believed that dreams had layers of symbolism that could be peeled away and decoded, making them powerful tools for understanding the world. They balanced this reverence with an appreciation for the way dreams often play with puns and riddles, celebrating the humor in dreams as well as their gravity. Priests served as dream interpreters, and people with vivid dreams were considered blessed.

The Egyptians built sanctuaries with rooms and special beds for dreaming. People went to these sacred places for advice, comfort, and healing, and to incubate specific dreams. It was believed that, while sleeping, one's spirit could shape-shift, taking the form of a bird or an animal to cross through time and space.

The ancient Egyptian hieroglyphic word for "dreaming" was depicted as an open eye, a symbol that also meant "awakening."

The Underworld was the home of the spirits of the dead, but it was also where dreams originated and a place dreamers could visit. Dreams were seen as a way to maintain contact with the deceased: People performed rituals and wrote letters to their departed loved ones to encourage visitation between realms. Sometimes, dead enemies would harass the living by bringing plagues of nightmares, and then the dreamer might ask a deceased loved one to intervene on their behalf and put an end to the bad dreams.

THE PHARAOH AND THE SPHINX

To this day, the Great Sphinx of Giza holds a stele—a stone tablet—between its paws, referencing the story of how this enormous statue came to be restored:

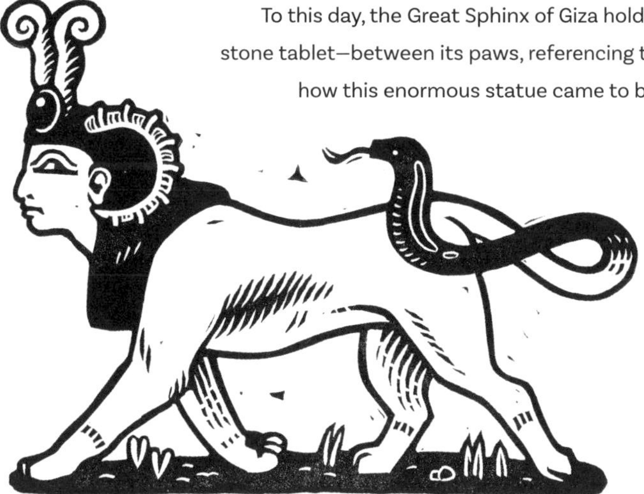

When he was still a young prince, Thutmose IV was out walking in the desert when he found himself in the shadow of the Sphinx. Although it was midday, he was suddenly overtaken by sleep. In a dream, the Sphinx—representing the sun god—offered Thutmose his earthly kingdom if he would repair the deteriorated statue. When he woke, Thutmose got straight to work, clearing sand to reveal the mighty Sphinx. His labor complete, the newly crowned Pharaoh Thutmose recorded his dream on a stele, placing it at the feet of his benefactor.

*The **Ramesside Dream Book** is an ancient Egyptian papyrus that lists more than two hundred dream meanings and classifies them as good or bad omens. It contains spells to counteract bad dreams, suggesting potions, amulets, herbs, and hymns to keep them at bay.*

ANCIENT GREECE AND ROME

"For those who are awake, there is a single, common universe, whereas in sleep each person turns away into his own, private universe."

—Heraclitus of Ephesus (Fragment 89)

Ancient Greeks had a complex relationship with dreams. While skeptical Greek philosophers, well-known for extolling the virtues of rationality, questioned their validity, dreams were nonetheless linked to mental, spiritual, and physical healing. Pilgrims would make arduous trips to temples of Asclepius, god of medicine, located high on mountaintops. Guided by dream-priests, they participated in rituals involving purification baths, prayer, and herbal concoctions. The seekers would fall asleep on designated cots to incubate divine dreams that would diagnose or even cure their ailments.

The philosopher **Artemidorus**, who lived centuries after Plato and Aristotle, dedicated his life to studying, collecting, and classifying dreams. He traveled the world, gathering personal dream accounts, interviewing interpreters and soothsayers for their insights, and compiling his findings in his great five-volume tome, the ***Oneirocritica***. Artemidorus believed that to fully understand a dream, the dreamer's background must be considered: A king dreaming about a sparrow means something different from a slave dreaming it, for instance, because a symbol's meaning relies heavily on its context.

ROMAN ADOPTION

Many ancient Greek practices were adopted and adapted under Roman rule, eventually developing into new traditions. The Roman emperor Augustus required that citizens bring any dreams they had about the state to the public marketplace and post them, presumably because this information was considered valuable to the community, should it represent a valid prophecy.

CLASSES OF DREAMS

(According to Artemidorus, later reworked by Pascalis Romanus)

- **ENHYPNIA:** Dreams about situations past and present.

    Insomnium: Dreams that reflect emotional and physical problems occurring in real life (stress dreams). Often based on physical or emotional disturbances, these are reflections and distortions of waking-life events.

    "A hungry man will dream of eating and a thirsty man will dream of drinking."

    Phantasma: Apparitions of little significance, with no basis in waking reality but also lacking prophetic meaning.

- **ONEIROI:** Prophetic dreams, or dreams about the future.

    Theorematic: Predictive dreams in which the outcome corresponds directly to the vision.

"A man out at sea dreamt that he was shipwrecked, and he did find himself in that situation: When sleep left him, the ship sank and was lost . . ."

    Allegorical: Predictive dreams, including riddles that must be decoded or symbols that require an interpreter.

- **Artemidorus** further divides allegorical dreams into five subcategories:

    Personal: dreams about oneself
    Other-party: dreams about someone else
    Double-reference: dreams involving the dreamer and someone else
    Public: dreams that occur in public places
    Cosmic: dreams that predict troubles in the order of the cosmos

"The total eclipse of the sun, moon, or other stars, or upheavals of earth or sea . . ."

CYCLE IV

THE SPIRIT

CYCLE IV WEEK 1 ○ NEW MOON

ACCESSING SPIRITUAL DEPTHS

In ancient Greece, the **Pythia**, also known as the **Oracle of Delphi**, was a priestess of the sun god Apollo, and she possessed the gift of prophecy. Above her temple were carved the words ***Know Thyself,*** a reminder to all who entered that, while the oracle could provide prophecy, the seeker must first know in their heart who they are before receiving divine guidance.

EXPLORE:

What does it mean to "know thyself"? Take some time to reflect on the questions below, jotting down a few thoughts in your journal.

* **What makes you . . . you?** Is it your values? Your possessions? Your personality? Your actions? Your relationships? Your beliefs? Having a body? Having thoughts, moods, or emotions?
* **What are your limitations, the things you won't do or can't believe?** Often what defines a thing are its edges, so one way to know ourselves is to figure out what we're *not*.
* **How have you changed throughout your life?** Are you recognizable to your past self? Many aspects of the self can change over time.
* **What aspects of yourself remain consistent?** What core traits have *not* changed since you were young?

DREAMS: THE EGALITARIAN ORACLE

According to Greek myth, the primordial Earth goddess Python gave mankind access to dreams as an act of revenge against Apollo, the god of prophecy, for usurping her home and power in Delphi. Python, a great serpent who lived underground, granted the gift of foresight to all humans in the form of dreams, which diminished Apollo's exclusive power over hints about what would happen in the future.

The fact that dreams appear to all regardless of age, IQ, or status bothered some of the ancient Greek philosophers. Plato mostly dismissed dreams as a kind of animalistic anarchy in which rational humans lost control of reason. His student, Aristotle, called it absurd that commoners and slaves received oracular visions rather than only the "best and wisest" of us.

CONSIDER:

Dreams can serve to spiritually metabolize the events of our daily lives. Just as the digestive system chews and churns food, extracting energy to power our bodies before eliminating the waste, dreaming can help us mentally and emotionally process our experiences.

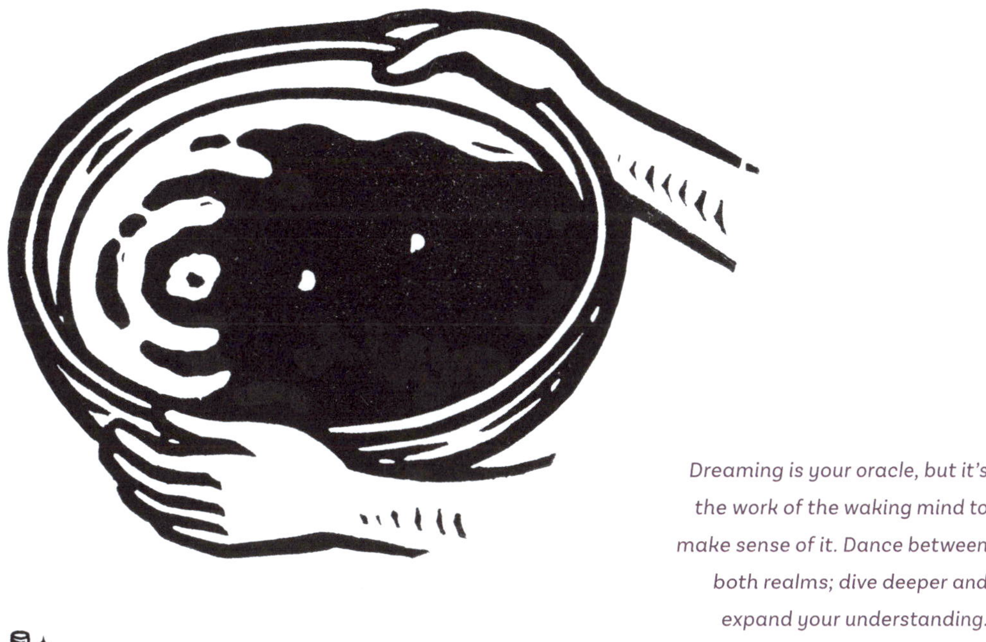

Dreaming is your oracle, but it's the work of the waking mind to make sense of it. Dance between both realms; dive deeper and expand your understanding.

CONJURE:

This week, try using your dreams as a tool to get to know yourself a little better.

Before you fall asleep, write a sentence in your dream journal expressing what you wish to discover. You may not know exactly what you're looking for, in which case you can write down something open-ended, like, "Dreams, show me who I am," or "What is my purpose?" or "Who is (your name)?" Alternatively, you can state this declaratively: "In my dreams tonight, I will learn something new about myself."

Tell yourself you will wake upon receiving this information, and you will remember it. In the morning, write down whatever insights your dream offered.

Later in the day, compare your daytime journal reflections from the "Explore" section above to the messages your dreams brought you.

CYCLE IV WEEK 2 WAXING MOON

CULTIVATING RITUAL

The English word "ritual" comes from the Latin *ritus* (meaning "rite") and refers to an act performed with an air of ceremony and significance. More than a habit, a ritual is elevated by a sense of the sacred. We use ritual to give our lives order and deeper meaning; we enact traditions that have been passed down through generations, and we create personal routines, marking significant events with deliberate actions. Rituals can be shared or individual, but there tends to be an element of repetition to them, whether they take place daily, annually, or in recognition of a significant occasion, such as death, birth, or marriage.

CONSIDER:

Reflect on the rituals in your life. What rituals do you perform on a regular basis? What about on special holidays or occasions? What family rituals have been passed down to you, and what rituals have you created for yourself?

PLAY:

Incorporate a ritual into one of your daily activities to turn an ordinary moment into something cherished.

Drinking your morning coffee, for example, is a habit or routine—but your outlook and intention can make it something more. By deliberately taking your mug to the porch and watching the sunrise, you can turn the habit into a small ritual.

Expand on this, infusing each step in your process with similar attention. Consider the coffee grounds and where they came from; take a moment to appreciate the water and the heat that transform these ground beans into a beverage that awakens you to a new day. As you watch the sunrise, honor this great star that gives us light and life.

How does your attitude and mindset shift when you decide you're performing a ritual?

In the evening, you can perform another ritual by going for a walk around the block after your supper, acknowledging the living things you encounter: plants, insects, and animals.

Nearly any routine action can become a ritual. It all depends on what you bring to it, what you believe it means, who joins you, and how seriously you choose to take it.

EXPLORE:

This week, experiment with creating a **personal dream ritual**. During last month's cycle, we explored different ways to activate the senses. Draw from those experiences and incorporate them into a ritual you can repeat on nights when you wish to focus on dreaming. By adding ceremony to your dreamwork, you imbue your practice with a sense of sacredness and importance.

Your dream ritual will be unique to you and will likely include a variety of elements. With repetition, you'll begin to associate the individual elements of your ritual with dreaming—a specific smell or sound alone might conjure that quality of mind you're trying to access.

HINT: *You may wish to adapt a simplified version of your ritual for nightly dreaming and create a more elaborate version for full moons or nights when you're seeking significant answers.*

Consider folding any of these actions into your dream ritual:

* Shower before bed, dousing the tub or shower floor with a few drops of lavender essential oil.
* Sip mugwort tea while observing the night sky.
* Place an herb-filled dream sachet under your pillow.
* Write down your dream intention, anoint it with oil, and tuck it into your pillowcase.
* Light incense and meditate on the curls of smoke.
* Lie down in darkness and listen to a specific song.
* Place a warm, damp washcloth or silken eye pillow over your eyes.
* Ring a bell or a gong before bed.
* Wear special pajamas.
* Greet your dream-self with a warm hello.
* Read a prayer, poem, or intention out loud.
* Draw a repetitive pattern in your dream journal.
* Perform a series of relaxing stretches.
* Pull a tarot or oracle card and meditate on its imagery and meaning.

CYCLE IV WEEK 3 ● FULL MOON

DREAM DEITIES

Many cultures believe that dreams come from an external spiritual source: the ancestors, divinity, the collective unconscious, or the universe itself. If that belief is not already a part of your worldview, spend some time reflecting on what it might mean to open yourself to a force beyond your individual self and consciousness.

On this full moon, direct some energy toward connecting with a **dream spirit**. You can find a list of dream deities from around the world on page 163, but feel free to research others or even summon your own. Look at images of them, make your own depictions, visualize them in your dreamworld, or pray or speak to them with a request for a significant or interesting dream.

If you are a religious practitioner and the themes of this week feel out of line with your beliefs, you may instead choose to connect with the practices of your religion before sleep. Keep in mind that dreams and dreaming are significant within each of the major world religions: Christianity, Islam, Hinduism, Judaism, and Buddhism. Many cultures also believe dreams are a way to connect to ancestors; maybe this speaks to you and invites further exploration.

If you find all of this dubious, use the activity as a thought experiment. Approach it with an open mind, and see if visualization has any effect on your dreams. You could also try thinking of a spirit as the personification of an **archetype** (see page 60): Imagine an abstract entity—an idea rather than a deity—that you give more shape and power to through attention and communication.

EXPLORE:

Write a message to a dream deity or your ancestors. Honor the spirit of dreaming by verbalizing what you appreciate about dreams, what you've gotten from them, and what you hope to receive as you continue your dreamwork practice.

Try sketching what you think the spirit of dreams looks like. Imagine what kinds of entities exist in the dream realm, how they might bring people dreams, and why.

You may want to make an offering to the dream spirit: Light a candle, fill a glass with water or wine for the spirit, sing a song, or recite an ode—a poem of praise.

HONORING THE FULL MOON

This week, perform the grandest embodiment of your dream ritual, taking some time to soak in the beauty of the moon at its fullest. Celebrate your ritual with all the air of a holiday: Anoint your head with dream oil, drink dream tea, read your intention out loud before falling asleep, and dress in full dream regalia!

Take all the best elements of the ritual you developed last week and use them to honor and celebrate dreams on this auspicious night.

CONJURE:

If you don't have a good grasp on the embodiment of a personal dream spirit, you can ask your dreams to introduce you.

Before bed, write in your dream journal: *I will meet the spirit of dreams tonight.* See who appears.

In the morning, write down anything that came to you in your dreams, knowing it might take a few nights of trying.

HINT: *Don't disregard whoever or whatever might appear, as your dream spirit could be something easily overlooked. Dreams are good at shifting shapes, after all.*

CONSIDER:

The universe is alive, and you are a part of it. How can you use your dreams to engage in dialogue with the cosmos?

REFLECT:

Open yourself to the idea that your dreams can help you navigate change, offering strength and wisdom as you maneuver through storms, and support you as you travel into deeper, uncharted waters.

Go back through your journal and create a dialogue with some of your past entries. Write questions and comments in the margins or beneath the lines of text:

- *What are you trying to tell me here?*
- *Did you mean . . . ?*
- *Thanks for this insight!*
- *Ah, you were trying to warn me about . . . !*

Have a little conversation.

CYCLE IV WEEK 4 WANING MOON

BEDSIDE AMBIENCE

This week, observe your sleep space: your room, your bed, your bedside table. Notice what you keep close. Your environment can influence the energy of your dreamwork, and if you change things up, you may notice subtle shifts in your dreaming.

Spend time this week curating the area near where you fall asleep. Pay attention to how you decorate and adorn your space, and observe the significance of the items you keep close. You may even decide to convert your bedside table into a **dream altar**.

EXPLORE:

A bedside altar can help imbue your sleep space with a sense of purpose. Decide on a general aesthetic you find inspiring, then add objects to elicit the vibe. You can rearrange, remove, or add items at different times, perhaps corresponding to the energies you wish to bring to your dreams.

Begin by laying down a piece of fabric on your bedside table. What might suggest the atmosphere you seek—a thick piece of dark velvet? Delicate hand-woven lace, or a square of bright, colorful cotton? Perhaps you'll choose a piece of plain cloth that you embroider or write on with fabric markers, forever preserving your dream intentions.

Once you have the cloth, add objects evoking the energy you're after. Anything that calls to you is welcome, but you might consider some of the items on this list:

* A figurine or image to represent dreaming
* Symbolic items: bones, dice, a key, a compass, items from nature
* Your dream journal
* Books about dreaming or a dream dictionary
* Dream oil
* Poetry—a book or a favorite poem written down
* Moonstone crystals, lapis lazuli, rose quartz, obsidian, or a stone special to you

NEXT, INCORPORATE THE ELEMENTS:

* **Water.** Place a glass of water on your table. Water has a strong connection to the dream realm (see page 161).
* **Fire.** Set up a candle. Any kind will do: a taper in a candlestick holder, a votive candle, a tea light, or whatever speaks to you. Light it ten minutes before bed and let it burn while you write your dream intention or reflect on past dream journal entries. Blow the candle out before you lay your head on the pillow to sleep for the night.
* **Earth.** Keep a living plant nearby, perhaps one of the herbs mentioned on page 33. Alternatively, arrange fresh or dried flowers, herbs, or grasses in a vase.
* **Air.** Display a beautiful fan or a feather, or open a window near your altar to let in the natural breeze.

CONSIDER:

Give some thought to your bed itself: its role and meaning in your life. It is your ship on the oneironautical journey, the vessel that carries you into the realm of dreams. It holds you while you sleep, when you are at your most vulnerable, and it is a place dedicated to rest, comfort, and peace. It's also a place for pleasure and love, and in times of illness, it may become a space of confinement, as well as recovery and restoration. Ideally, your bed is where you will make your transition at the end of life to whatever comes next. This is a sacred place, a sanctuary: Honor and appreciate how it supports you.

PLAY:

Wreaths have been used throughout history to represent natural cycles and their renewal. Ancient Greek laurel wreaths were worn to denote high status. Scandinavian harvest wreaths were created as offerings. Protective wreaths were hung on doors to keep bad luck at bay, and to this day we lay funereal wreaths on graves and hang festive wreaths to mark holidays. You can continue this tradition by weaving a **dream wreath** from plants associated with sleep.

Mugwort (page 33), for example, is a fragrant plant that grows wild and abundantly out of rocky, dry earth. It has long been associated with dreams and is said to promote lucid dreaming, vivid dreams, and dream recall. Its Latin name, *Artemisia*, comes from Artemis—the Greek goddess of the moon.

If you can find mugwort growing (look by train tracks, empty lots, and other commonly overgrown areas), gather some by cutting a few stalks down near the base of the plant. Shake out any loose seeds to help propagate a new season of life.

You can easily bend your mugwort stalks into a ring. To give your wreath a little more structure, wrap string, twine, or ribbon around it. You can also weave in other dream-related herbs, like rosemary, chamomile, or lavender.

Hang your wreath near or above your bed and the fragrance of the herbs will contribute to your dreaming atmosphere.

CHECK IN:

You've completed a few months of dreamwork now. Review your intentions and ask yourself how you feel about them. Take some time to read through your dream journal and reflect on your experiences so far. Do another round of typing up your dreams or rewriting them by hand in neater script. This will be especially useful in the months ahead, as we'll begin sifting through past dreams: metabolizing, interpreting, and embodying them. As you review your dreams, consider these questions:

* *Do you notice any patterns emerging?*
* *Have you had any new or interesting experiences in your dreams since you've begun incorporating ritual into your practice? (Revisit the list on page 47.)*
* *Have your dreams changed in terms of their quality? Are they any more vivid or remarkable?*

If you haven't noticed much change, give yourself space to accept this and recommit to your plan. Keep going and trust the process.

DREAMING JOURNEY:
RELIGIOUS PERSPECTIVES

THE PROPHETS

Dreaming played a major role in the development and spread of most of the major religions of the modern world. The Jewish, Christian, and Islamic holy books all tell stories of men who had divine dreams: Jacob, Abraham, Joseph, Moses, and Noah in the Torah or Old Testament, and Muhammad in the Qur'an. It was the duty of these prophets, as messengers of God, to interpret and share their divine dreams with the public, and in doing so, recruit followers.

JUDAISM AND CHRISTIANITY

Jacob, a Hebrew patriarch, used a stone as a pillow and dreamed of a staircase leading into the sky. A voice told him that the land on which he lay would belong to him and his descendants, who would be "as numerous as the stars." When he woke, Jacob pledged his life to Yahweh and reenacted his dream by building a stone pillar that reached to the heavens.

Jacob's son **Joseph** was even more well-known for his relationship with dreams, being a naturally skilled dream interpreter. Joseph's dreams were full of symbolism and poetry, but when he repeatedly had dreams suggesting that his older brothers should bow down to him, his siblings, infuriated, threw him into a pit and left him for dead.

"What good are his dreams now?" they joked.

Joseph was able to escape, though he was soon captured, sold into slavery, and later imprisoned in Egypt. In jail, he interpreted the dreams of his fellow inmates, predicting that in three days' time, one would get his job back and the other would be executed. When the one who got his job back told the pharaoh about Joseph's skill, the pharaoh freed Joseph and appointed him royal dream interpreter.

The pharaoh shared with Joseph that he had been plagued by a series of concerning dreams: seven skinny cows eating seven fat cows, followed by a dream of seven skinny ears of corn devouring seven plump ears of corn. Jacob proposed that these dreams meant there would be seven years of abundance followed by seven years of famine. The pharaoh heeded Joseph's interpretation: During the years of plenty, he put stores aside for the future so his people wouldn't starve.

The story of Joseph illustrates how prophetic dreams offer guidance when the future is uncertain. These specific dreams also show the importance of numerical symbolism—in this case, the correlation between numbered objects and time.

ISLAM

In 610 CE in Saudi Arabia, forty-year-old **Muhammad** left his family for a monthlong spiritual retreat in a cave on Mount Hira—a common practice among the polytheistic people of the region. One night, as he slept in the cave, Muhammad was visited by the angel **Gabriel**, who proclaimed, "*Iqra!*" (meaning "recite") and woke him from his sleep. The word echoing in his mind, Muhammad puzzled over what the message meant on a deeper level. When he left the cave, he saw that Gabriel had taken the form of the entire sky and horizon. The angel was everywhere, and he told Muhammad that he would be the apostle of Allah.

Muhammad obeyed Gabriel's message and spent the rest of his life spreading the word of Allah. Throughout this time, he received many other divine dreams and visions, weaving together stories also found in Jewish and Christian scripture.

His followers memorized his teachings, shared them, and wrote them down, creating the Qur'an. Just like the Torah and the New Testament, the Qur'an suggests that dreams are a communication tool between the human and the divine.

HINDUISM

Dreams appear repeatedly in the **Vedas** and the **Upanishads**, ancient holy texts of Hinduism. According to Hindu belief, both dreams and the waking life are illusions created by the god **Vishnu**—in fact, dreaming and deep sleep are considered more important states than being awake.

In Hinduism, dreams are understood to have a psychological component. They reveal inner desires, and they also possess the mystical ability to predict the future and influence the present. Often, they are tools to cleanse and heal the mind. However, they are not always abstractions that warrant interpretation. Several Hindu texts describe dreams themselves as objects: weapons that can be used to attack an adversary, for example, or token-like charms that can protect the dreamer.

BUDDHISM

The story of **Siddhartha Gautama**, the Buddha, begins with a dream experienced by his mother, **Queen Maya**. She had attended the seven-day midsummer festival, and on the final day, she wore her finest clothes, ate sacred food, distributed alms, and performed the rites of the holy day. She took a perfumed bath before falling asleep for the night. That night, under the full moon, Maya dreamt of a white elephant holding a white lotus flower in its trunk. The elephant circled her three times, then entered her womb. Nine months later, she gave birth to a prince, Siddhartha Gautama.

But Siddhartha was not content living his princely life of luxury, and he eventually abandoned the palace in search of deeper truth. He sat under the Bodhi Tree on his birthday, under a full moon, and vowed to stay there until he discovered the meaning of life. Throughout the night, he was tormented by a demon named **Mara**, who was determined to force him to move—or at the very least, to distract him. Mara's efforts failed, however, and when dawn rose, Siddhartha had become enlightened: He had become the Buddha.

Because of the importance of dreaming in the story of the Buddha, dreams are held in high regard as tools that offer spiritual insight. Still, they are considered inferior to true enlightenment, a state of transcendent spiritual consciousness that Buddhists strive for.

JAINISM

In the Jain religion, fourteen things a pregnant woman might dream of are considered highly auspicious for her child. Dreaming of the moon, for instance, predicts that the child-to-be will bring peace and help to others; a pair of fish denotes handsomeness; dreaming of a heap of jewels indicates the baby will possess abundant wealth: material, intellectual, moral, and spiritual. If a mother dreams all fourteen symbols during her pregnancy, it is said that her child will grow up to be the universal monarch.

THE DANGER OF DREAMING

Despite the foundational role dreams play in many of the world's major religions, they were also seen as a potential threat as the monotheistic religions became more established. Since dreaming comes naturally to all humans, it was risky for people in power to allow dreams to continue having such unfettered sway over important events. If *anyone* could have a divine dream, some dreams might threaten those in power. Religious leaders questioned the validity of dreams and asserted that many nightly visions came from a demonic rather than a divine source, even going so far as to claim that Satan himself was attempting to trick or tempt people in their sleep. These leaders were not above using violence and intimidation to reinforce their message.

In medieval Europe, vivid dreams—along with anything perceived as witchcraft or heresy—became punishable by death. The war against heresy and pagan beliefs was an effective instrument of control later wielded by missionaries and colonizers during imperialist conquests across Europe and the Americas in the fifteenth century, and in Africa during the nineteenth century. Naturally, Indigenous people began to guard their dreaming experiences. However, much knowledge from cultures with robust dreaming traditions is lost to history, as their practitioners were converted, enslaved, conquered, or killed.

CYCLE V

THE PSYCHE

DREAM PSYCHOLOGY

In the early twentieth century, an Austrian doctor named **Sigmund Freud** proposed a science to dreaming. This was revolutionary at the time—at least, to the few who didn't dismiss Freud's theory as nonsense.

Freud, now known as the founder of **psychoanalysis**, was fascinated by the workings of human consciousness. Through interviews with his patients, Freud hypothesized that dreams were the brain's way of processing the stress and traumas of our lives. He encouraged his patients to use **free association**: to speak without a filter and allow ideas to flow. This process, he claimed, allowed repressed thoughts to surface. By analyzing dreams, people could gain insight into their problems and better address them. Today, this remains a widely accepted theory of dreaming.

Freud argued that dreams could be categorized into two groups based on their origins. Dreams that came "from above"—also called **day residues**—are caused by thoughts, concerns, and activities that have seeped from daily life into the dreamworld. These are the dreams populated by people and activities we commonly encounter in our day-to-day lives. Dreams that come "from below" grow from the formative, unconscious desires that took root during infancy and are a form of **wish fulfillment**. Freud believed that dreams "from below" hold far more influence.

It's important to note that while Freud was heavily inspired by ideas and concepts from Indigenous cultures, he, like his peers, generally regarded these people as "primitive." Other criticisms of Freud acknowledge the ways his biases and neuroses prevented him from being fully objective in his work. His particular obsessions with childhood, sexuality, and the family's influence on individual development may have limited his exploration of the full range of human experience and the wider array of factors that contribute to it. All the same, his attention to dreams and his insight into human behavior significantly impacted our modern understanding of dreaming and human psychology.

WISH FULFILLMENT

Freud famously posited that dreams can serve as vehicles for wish fulfillment: The things we dream about are the things we want. Even the subjects that frighten, disturb, or disgust us in our dreams arise from a kind of perverse desire in the dark depths of our minds that can be traced back to infancy.

Freud also developed a theory of **repression**: If you push something away or deny it, it'll find new ways to rear its head.

EXPLORE:

Dreams capture the intricate, messy possibilities of our lives, showing us parallel universes where we get the things we want and face the things that frighten us. This week, spend some time naming and observing your wishes and desires—without judgment or expectation.

Dreams have a habit of bringing to light the deeper, bigger questions we don't have the capacity to address in waking life. Spending some time with as-of-yet unfulfilled wishes—either through thought, meditation, or dreams—can help us move toward acceptance or action rather than letting these desires consume us in unhealthy ways.

In your dream journal, write down the things you most want in life. Don't be afraid to express your deepest desires, even if you're embarrassed to admit them. Desire can be very complex; it's not always as straightforward as "I want [X], so I'm going to work hard to get it." This exercise is for you. Push away any feelings of shame, silliness, or ambivalence, and allow yourself the space to name what you want.

Worry, like wishing, is a way of channeling mental energy toward a particular outcome; it just has a more negative focus.

REFLECT:

Page back through your journal and look for dreams that made you uncomfortable. Try framing them as Freud would, in terms of wish fulfillment: *How might this unsettling dream be fulfilling a secret desire of mine?*

DREAMS AND TRAUMA

During World War I, frontline hospitals were filled with soldiers suffering from **shell shock**—psychological trauma caused by their experiences in combat. To treat them, European doctors experimented with Freud's newly developed talk therapy and dream interpretation, encouraging the soldiers to share their dreams and write them down as poems. In doing so, the traumatized men found a way to express and release some of the indescribable horrors that haunted them.

Aware of this work, Freud amended his theory that all dreams fulfill a wish, concluding that **traumatic dreams** were an exception to the rule. Later, however, he shifted his position once more, proposing that nightmares of past trauma are, in fact, still a form of wish fulfillment: They represent a desire to relive traumatic events so that a person can overcome them.

DREAMING TOWARD THE COLLECTIVE

Carl Jung is probably as well-known in the fields of psychology and dream studies as his mentor, Dr. Freud. Jung, a Swiss doctor, was fascinated by Freud's ideas and used them as a springboard for his own theories. He employed a holistic model that saw dreams as tools for leading a fuller, richer life, focusing on their potential to connect us to a sense of collectivity.

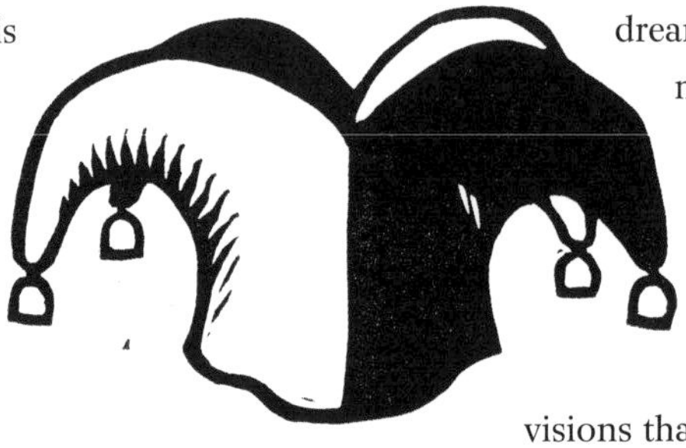

To this day, we still use many of Jung's terms to define elements of the dreaming world. However, as with Freud's writing, we can find earlier evidence of these concepts across many different cultures, suggesting they were not original to these men but innate human experiences.

JUNGIAN TERMS AND CONCEPTS

Jung developed a theory of the **collective unconscious**: the deep, primal well of energy and thought that transcends personal experience. The collective unconscious is inherited and accessible to all humans. Jung believed our dreams connect us spiritually to one another and that we can find a deeper understanding of ourselves by working through them.

Jung was also fascinated by what he called **Big Dreams**: significant visions distinguished from regular dreams by their divine or mystical nature. Although these kinds of dreams don't happen frequently, many people experience them at some point in their lives, and cultures around the world acknowledge their profound importance: These are the visions that leave us with a sense of wonder and awe upon waking.

Big Dreams occur more often during times of transition, such as adolescence and midlife, periods of grief, moments of success or failure, pregnancy (or a partner's pregnancy), and in the days or weeks leading up to death. They also appear with greater frequency to people experiencing psychosis, and they can often accompany significant self-work. (We will work more closely with Big Dreams in Cycle VI, Week 3.)

Jung is also responsible for our current understanding of the term **archetype**, used in psychology to describe universal characters that appear in global myths, art, narratives, and individual dreams. The following list of Jungian archetypes isn't definitive; there are certainly more, and they can vary across cultures.

CAREGIVER	**INNOCENT**
HEALER	**EVERYMAN**
KING	**REBEL**
HERO	**OTHER**
FOOL	**SAGE**
VILLAIN/ADVERSARY	**MAGICIAN**
LOVER	**SERVANT**
BEAST	**CREATOR**
TRICKSTER	**JUDGE**

Can you think of any other archetypes you're familiar with?

When archetypes appear in our dreams, they are probably trying to communicate something important. What might this character be telling you? Do you need more of that energy in your life? Are you afraid of or irritated by it?

The archetype, and all Jungian work, is meant to help the individual explore their sense of self more deeply by situating them within the context of the greater collective—helping them come to peace with who they are by facing, questioning, and appreciating it.

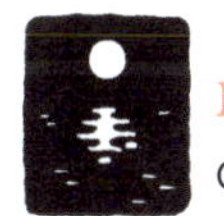

REFLECT:

Comb through your dream journal in search of archetypes. When you come across one by name, circle it. Pay close attention to dreams with people in them. Could they be representing certain archetypes? Does looking at your dreams from this perspective change or deepen their meaning?

When a person from your waking life appears in a dream, they may be more of a stand-in or symbol for an archetype, trying to tell you something about yourself or your position in life

EXPLORE:

Look for examples of archetypes in media and in your daily life, noting them in your journal.

Notice how complicated and complex a living, breathing human is, even when they might seem to fully embody a certain archetype. For instance, a teacher can represent the Sage archetype—but if they don't know their material, they might also be playing the role of the Fool. If they're a rigid authoritarian in the classroom, they might represent the Adversary to some of their students. And when making dinner for their family at home, they may embody the Caregiver. In this way, each of us reflects and expresses a multitude of archetypes depending on context.

***Tarot cards** make use of archetypes. In a tarot reading, when a card is reversed, it means the energy of that card's archetype is blocked, delayed, or poorly placed—for example, a reversed King might be a tyrant rather than a fair ruler.*

CONSIDER:

According to Jungian theory, each of us contains all the archetypes to varying degrees. To fully understand ourselves, we must accept and embrace our many different aspects, even those that make us most uncomfortable.

Which archetypes do you identify with intuitively? Which do you reject or dislike—and why? We will spend more time with these "negative" aspects next week when we dive into shadow work.

PLAY:

Your **persona** is the self you present outwardly.

Is your persona in line with your inner self?

*

Does the face you show the world hide certain aspects of yourself or exaggerate others?

*

Does your persona change depending on the audience, environment, or occasion?

Pay attention to your persona this week and play around with it some. See how it feels to harmlessly "act" a little differently. According to Jung, clothing is a meaningful element of persona. Notice what you're wearing in your dreams, as this might provide insight into the roles you're playing—in dreams and perhaps in life. Take note of masks, costumes, hair, disguises, props, or other vestments through which your persona might reveal itself to you in dreamland.

CYCLE V WEEK 3 ● FULL MOON

THE SHADOW

Shadow work is the practice of uncovering and coming to terms with the parts of ourselves we try to hide or reject. According to Jung's theory of archetypes, each of us has a shadow-self, unless you're perfect—in which case you have a lot of shadow work to do, because you're living in denial!

*Accepting the multifaceted nature of your whole self is called **integration** and is a primary goal of Jung's psychotherapy work.*

EXPLORE:

To engage in shadow work, you'll need to examine yourself honestly, without getting too bogged down in self-doubt or self-hatred. As objectively as you can, reflect on the prompts below, responding in your dream journal.

* What qualities do you wish you could change in yourself, and why?
* What do these same qualities provide for you? What uses do they serve?
* Are there any other ways you could receive that support?
* How do these qualities impact the people around you? How do they impact *you*?
* How can you demonstrate compassion for your shadow-self?
* How can you relinquish some of your shadow's power over you so you can grow?

GO DEEPER

Sometimes we project the things we hate or fear most onto others, so if someone in your life is a source of great agitation, try to figure out what, specifically, bothers you about them. Write down the person's name and their qualities that irritate you. Examine your own life and personality, speculating on why those particular traits grate on you so much. How do these same qualities appear in you?

Balance this exercise by finding and naming at least one quality you can appreciate in the person who annoys you.

CONJURE:

Use your dreams as a mirror. Ask them to send you a visit from your shadow. The reflection you receive might be distorted, but perhaps it can reveal truths you haven't been ready to face.

Try to remain curious and open to any distressing characters you encounter in your dreams; see if you can learn something from them.

Who asks for a stressful dream? It might not make for the most restful sleep, but an intentional dream encounter with your shadow may help you move through emotional blockages. Try this on a night when you don't have looming responsibilities the next day!

CONSIDER:

The things we push away, hide, or deny are often things we feel negatively about. However, sometimes we also repress or avoid things that are too beautiful or transcendent for us to accept. Dreams can help us uncover the secrets we try to hide from ourselves to function in waking life. When we're exposed to these secrets in small doses, as in dreams, we can become more comfortable with them.

REFLECT:

Review your dream entries and look for places where your shadow-self may have made an appearance. The shadow might appear as an antagonist of some kind—a monster, a wild beast, or another destructive force or entity. Sometimes, it appears as a literal shadow.

Note that your persona—your public-facing self—is a mask, and your shadow is a projection. Neither of these represents your whole self, but they are two aspects of something much more complex. By observing the multiple, sometimes contradictory, facets of your self, you can get closer to understanding who you truly are.

Now, practice extending this grace to others in your life.

PLAY:

This week, play with literal shadows! Stand under a streetlight at night and appreciate the ways it exaggerates and distorts your silhouette; move your body and marvel at the shapes you cast.

Other ideas:

- Choreograph a shadow dance.
- Turn your shadow into an animal.
- Photograph your shadow. Trace it. Give it permanence.
- Draw a depiction of your shadow-self.

CHECK IN:

By now, you may have noticed your dreams becoming more vivid and memorable, especially if that was one of your goals. From here, your dreams will likely get longer and more intricate, and your memory of them will improve—which, ironically, makes it more difficult to record them in the morning.

Recommit to documenting your dreams, but don't feel like you need to spend hours doing so. As your dreams become more detailed, you may need to adjust your approach and find new methods for documenting them. Perhaps you jot down a few keywords to jog your memory later, or maybe you decide to focus on a single scene from your dream. Your approach will depend on what you hope to achieve; choose a technique that suits your particular goals.

PARADOXICAL DREAMS

Dreams don't always mean what we expect them to. In many cultures, dreaming of one thing might foreshadow its opposite in your waking life. In Chinese culture, for example, dreaming about death can portend great success, while dreaming about winning the lottery might warn of sudden bankruptcy. According to Irish superstition, when a pregnant woman dreams she's going to have a baby boy, she's probably going to have a girl. In African American culture, dreaming about a death foretells a birth, since one soul leaving means another one is making its entrance.

One explanation for paradoxical dreams is that in situations of peak intensity, energy begins to shift back toward the opposite pole in an attempt to find balance. Another theory is that the dreaming realm offers these visions to help us imagine alternate realities.

CYCLE V WEEK 4 ◐ WANING MOON

INTERPRETING SYMBOLS

If dreaming is a language, symbols are some of its most colorful, expressive words.

Interpreting symbols is an important element of dreamwork; however, it's often a very personal one. While you might be tempted to consult a **dream dictionary**—a straightforward, alphabetized list of symbols and their meanings—and be done with it, that isn't necessarily the most useful way to approach this kind of translation.

Say you dream about a bird. While a dream dictionary might say the bird symbolizes "freedom," you'll need a lot more information to truly understand what the bird means *to you*. Dream symbolism is highly subjective; a crow that appears in your dream will have a different meaning than a crow that appears in your grandfather's dream. Furthermore, dreaming of a crow means something different from dreaming of a vulture, a wren, or a toucan. Where was the bird? What was it doing? What personal connections do you have with this species?

Context is essential when deciphering symbols in a dream. For the most part, you'll want to look at the whole story within your dream and figure out how it relates to your life. Often, it's helpful to explore the dream's overarching themes—struggle, pursuit, getting lost, etc.—to understand its significance to you. But sometimes individual symbols can be the key to unlocking a grander narrative.

EXPLORE:

Because symbols are so contextual, it can be helpful to create a **personal symbol dictionary**, defining images, objects, and motifs according to your own insights and experiences. Try to focus on the feelings, memories, and meanings each symbol holds for you.

* Begin by turning to the back of your dream journal and counting out the last twenty-six pages. Alphabetize the pages by writing a letter at the top of each.
* Now, read through the entries in your dream journal, listing significant images or objects on the alphabetized pages."
* If you see a particular symbol more than once, mark a tally next to that entry.
* Finally, fill in your dictionary with possible meanings–but unlike a regular dictionary, these definitions are more like suggestions. What might each of these symbols mean to you personally? Consider your past experiences with each object, your emotional reaction to it, or any other associations that come to mind.

Refer to your personal symbol dictionary as often as you like. It can help you keep track of recurring motifs and decode their significance within your psychic landscape.

GO DEEPER

If you're struggling to define your symbols, or if you simply want to take a more visual approach, try "mapping" them instead.

Choose an image or object from your dream journal that you think could have some symbolic significance. Dreams often have what's called a **central symbol**: the main subject and focus of the dream.

Write the word you've chosen at the center of a clean page in your journal. Without necessarily thinking of the dream it appeared in, ask yourself what other words it calls to mind.

Set a timer for one to three minutes and write as many related words as you can, each branching away from your central word. For example, if your central word is "boat," you might write "sail," "water," "leaky," "pirate," "capsize," "holiday," or any number of other words.

HINT: *The connections between words don't have to make logical sense; this is your personal map. Trust that these associations surfaced for a reason.*

When the timer goes off, take a moment to admire your map. Do any of the words you chose surprise you? Perhaps your map offers an insight you wish to include in your personal symbol dictionary, or perhaps it sheds light on the dream in which your symbol appeared.

CONSIDER:

Apophenia is the human tendency to find patterns and connections between things. Our brains are naturally skilled at linking two seemingly disparate things; no matter how random, we can usually find some way to connect them, and it brings pleasure to do so. This tendency is useful in an evolutionary sense: We learn from our mistakes and successes, noticing outcomes so we can predict what will happen and either replicate or avoid certain results.

In the universe of dreams, everything is connected, and it can be deeply rewarding to seek and identify patterns.

REFLECT:

Yet another way to work with dream symbols is by asking questions about them and following where they lead. For example, if you dreamt of a pineapple, you can ask: *How big was it? Did it look fresh? Where did it come from? What was my emotional reaction to it? How did I interact with it? What personal memories do I have of pineapples?* A self-interview like this may offer a different kind of insight than free association.

You might follow this up by doing some research: A quick dive into the history of pineapples, for instance, reveals that they were a highly coveted trade item during colonial times—which could potentially offer a complex new level of meaning to your dream.

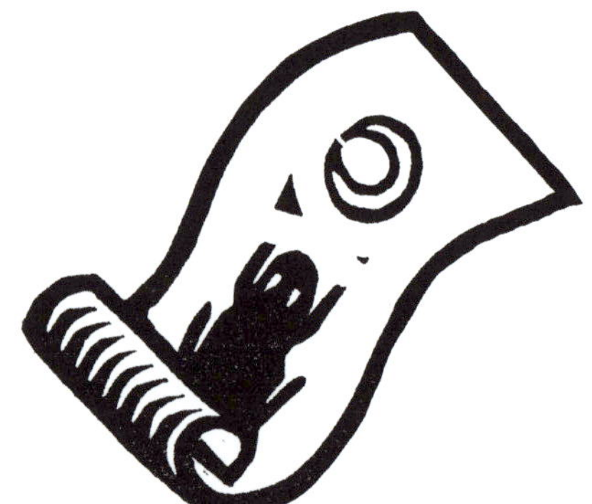

PLAY:

Dream dictionaries can be fun to use, even if their one-size-fits-all nature isn't always helpful. Sometimes they can add an unexpected element to your interpretation—something you never would have thought of on your own.

Find at least two dream dictionaries at your local library or bookshop and try your hand at this straightforward style of analysis:

* Choose a dream from your journal and circle the important objects or images. Look these symbols up in one of the dictionaries and write the definition below your entry.
* Next, consult the other dictionary, noting that meaning alongside the other.
* Compare the two: Do these translations tell different stories? Do either of them resonate with you?

DREAMING JOURNEY:

DREAMS AND SCIENCE

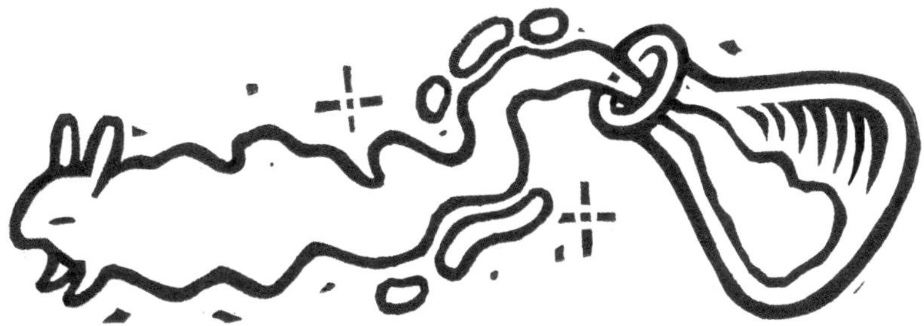

As cultures throughout time have observed, there exist different types of dreams, and in modern times, scientists have attempted to classify and better understand them. Some dreams are clearly processing the events of daily life, while others reflect deep psychological fears and desires. Still other dreams seem to have uncanny predictive or even mystical qualities, while some are simply beautiful and poetic—or seem like nonsense. Many dreams contain aspects of multiple types, depending on interpretation.

NEUROPHYSIOLOGICAL AND PSYCHOLOGICAL MODELS

From a holistic perspective, the body and mind are inextricably linked. Some of the theories put forth by dream researchers prioritize the biological processes within the brain, while others are interested in the ways dreams influence and define the individual and the collective unconscious.

By exploring some of the ideas others have put forward to explain dreaming, you can determine which models best fit your own understanding.

ACTIVATION-SYNTHESIS MODEL

In the late 1970s, scientists **Allan Hobson** and **Robert McCarley** theorized that dreaming is a purely mechanical process: the result of neurons firing while we sleep. Dreams, according to this model, are helpful for regulating brain health but don't have any deeper meaning. They are a secondary effect, like the heat a light bulb emits while it shines. Using EEG machines and other technology, Hobson and McCarley mapped what happens physically during the cycles of sleep, noting that the parts of the brain responsible for emotions and visualization are most active, and the prefrontal cortex, which controls thought, is more dormant. The **activation-synthesis model** posits that our brains must stay active even while we're asleep, and dreams are the by-product of these random brain signals. Any meaning we ascribe to them upon waking is our conscious mind's attempt to draw connections—to make sense out of nonsense.

MEMORY CONSOLIDATION, OR THE REVERSE LEARNING MODEL

A theory developed by **Francis Crick** and **Graeme Mitchison** in 1983, the **reverse learning model**, suggests that dreaming helps us practice and process things we've experienced in our waking lives, integrating daily skills and activities into our long-term memory. While we sleep, our brain reviews the events of the day and forms associations that our waking mind didn't quite complete, or it replays information to secure its place in our memory. For example, if you spent the evening learning how to knit, you might dream about knitting, reenacting the motions from earlier. People who dream about a new task they're learning tend to improve more quickly than people who don't. (See the ***Tetris* effect**, page 75.) According to the **memory consolidation model**, dreaming is a form of metabolism, the mental equivalent of digestion: The brain processes the data it's taken in, keeping what might be potentially useful and storing it as memory—and it discards what it decides won't be needed later.

PRIMITIVE INSTINCT REHEARSAL THEORY

The **primitive instinct rehearsal theory** suggests that the brain is sharpening its survival reflexes by practicing skills while we sleep. Since how we respond to a threat can influence our ability to survive, we need to be ready to identify risk and respond quickly and appropriately. This theory of instinct argues that our brains use sleep to practice scenarios so we know how to respond when we're faced with waking-life threats, much like a training tutorial.

WISH FULFILLMENT

Sigmund Freud, the originator of this theory, believed dreams allow us to experience the things we most desire, if only temporarily. These desires are rooted in childhood urges, and our mind conjures them in our dreams to keep us comforted so we stay asleep (see page 58).

EMOTIONAL REGULATION

In the **emotional regulation** model, dreams help take the edge off traumatic and stressful situations by allowing us to experience these moments of intensity in a passive, temporary way, free of physical pain. In this way, we can better heal from and tolerate life's stresses and traumas, big and small.

This model is connected to the activation-synthesis model but applies a more holistic framework: Dream research pioneer **Rosalind Cartwright** proposed, tested, and proved that the things we dream about are often reflections of the things we think about during the day. By studying the dreams of depressed people going through divorce, she discovered that people who have nightmares tend to recover from emotional pain more quickly than people who don't dream about their situation. Dreams, according to her findings, aid in emotional regulation and help us form a unified sense of self.

PROBLEM SOLVING

This model suggests that during dream sleep, regions of the brain associated with logic and impulse control are suppressed, while centers for abstraction and association are more engaged. The dreaming brain is therefore primed to make connections between disparate things, which is helpful for coming up with innovative solutions. With our conscious defenses down and our ingrained habits put on hold, dreams can offer a fresh way of understanding something our rational mind wouldn't bother entertaining.

CYCLE VI

STRANGE EXPERIENCES

CYCLE VI WEEK 1 NEW MOON

THRESHOLDS AND BOUNDARIES

One of the defining characteristics of the dream realm is its loose boundaries. Walls can be porous, objects mutable, the edges of reality thrumming and shifting. Things transform before our eyes, and we roll with it. This disorientation is part of what makes dreams so hard to hold on to once we wake up.

Boundaries—and what lies between and beyond them—are a part of the spectrum of consciousness, too. **Hypnagogia**, also known as threshold consciousness, is a state of awareness between sleep and waking. It's most commonly experienced right before a person falls asleep and again upon waking (although, then, it's sometimes referred to as **hypnopompia**).

EXPLORE:

Spending extended time in the hypnagogic state can offer more control over your dreams, potentially allowing you to direct them toward things you wish to explore.

HINT: *It's not easy to linger in a hypnagogic state if you're awakened abruptly, so it's best to play with hypnagogia on mornings when you don't have to jump out of bed right away.*

To encourage hypnagogia, remain still upon waking, your eyes closed. Don't bother writing down your dream. Instead, try to continue it; this is called **reentering** a dream. This time, rather than immersing yourself fully, try to be present as a witness.

Notice where you are and explore your surroundings. This might take you out of the hypnagogic state and into a more alert state, or you might fall back asleep without meaning to. It could also lead you to lucid dreaming, which we'll explore a little more deeply in Cycle X.

Without putting too much pressure on the activity, try this as often as you can this week.

PLAY:

In your journal, list out the groups, roles, or other categories you identify with. For example: human, Irish, American, queer, man, disabled, poet, nurse, father, son, etc.

How easy is it to put yourself in these boxes? Do you feel more comfortable existing in between or on the margins of them? While labels and identifiers can be useful and positive, they can also sow division, hurt, or discrimination.

Now, use your imagination to playfully hop outside the boxes you've listed. Pretend you belong to different categories or identities. For example, if you wrote down "woman" as one of your identifiers, imagine being a man, or a child—just as a thought experiment. "Human"? Write a sentence or two as a cat or a mushroom.

Imagine transgressing the boundaries that define you for a moment; the point is to play with the limits we perceive.

PARTIAL AROUSALS

Brief awakenings that most often occur during hypnagogia.

- **HYPNAGOGIC JERK:** The body or a part of it spasms reflexively; sometimes this can startle us awake.

- ***TETRIS* EFFECT:** When we've spent time learning something new or engaged in a repetitive task during the day, we have a tendency to replicate this activity while in the hypnagogic state. After hours of driving cross-country, for instance, we might see the open road when we close our eyes.

  This phenomenon gets its name from studies conducted on players of *Tetris*, a video game in which players try to neatly stack cubed shapes as they slide down the screen. After playing the game for extended periods of time, test subjects consistently reported seeing *Tetris* shapes fall when they closed their eyes in the moments before sleep. Players who experienced the game in a threshold state had improved scores the next time they played in waking life.

- **AUDITORY HALLUCINATIONS:** We might hear things that aren't there, like dripping water or murmured voices.

- **SLEEP PARALYSIS:** This can be a frightening experience, especially for someone who has never encountered it before. Typically, it involves a sense that the body is frozen or weighed down and the sleeper has no control over it. While sleep paralysis doesn't exclusively occur during hypnagogic threshold states, it's much more common then.

  Many cultures attribute sleep paralysis to demons. For example, in Catalonian folklore, a pesanta *is an enormous black-haired dog with steel claws that enters people's homes at night, sitting on their chests so they can't move or breathe.* *(See also: the Mara, page 158.)*

  Physiologically, sleep paralysis is explained as dysregulation caused by interrupted REM sleep. Remember that during REM, the body is paralyzed, so if we partially awaken during this time, we won't be able to control our body right away.

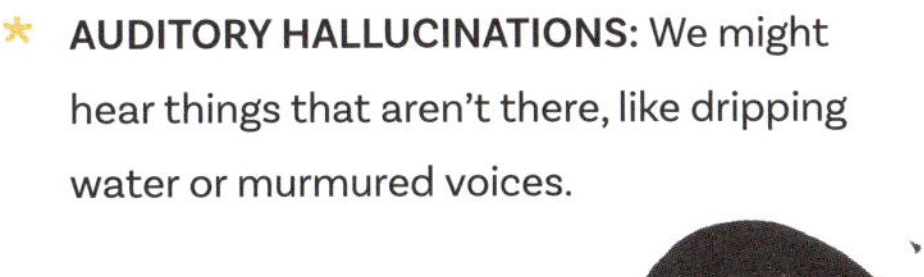

CONSIDER:

Consider the physical thresholds and boundaries of your waking world: walls, doors, bridges, archways, county lines, even the temporal thresholds between night and day—dusk and dawn. Pay attention to times when you move through these thresholds: when you step into a different town, open a door into another room, or when you find you need to turn on the light because evening has settled in. Look for places that exist on the outskirts or between two distinct locations—the edge of a quiet neighborhood bumping into an industrialized area, or a woodland transitioning into meadow.

Turn these times and places of transition into sites of simple ritual by giving them a moment of attention; mark the ending of one thing as it turns into the beginning of another. See if you can extend your time in the in-betweens: Notice the qualities of these places and times and what effect they have on you. Consider what transformations are happening inside you as you move through them; you, too, are always changing.

REFLECT:

How you manage your personal boundaries can influence how you dream and what you remember afterward.

Psychoanalyst and sleep researcher **Ernest Hartmann** posited that one's perceived separation from and connection to others—one's boundaries—influence dreaming. According to his studies, people with thinner boundaries—those whose sense of self, for example, is more fluid—report better dream recall. That's not to say we should aim to relax all boundaries, especially if we've put work into establishing them, but it's an interesting fact.

As with most things in life, balance is key. Our relationship to boundaries and thresholds is very likely linked to our feelings of control and surrender (see page 132). In your journal this week, think about your own personal boundaries: When have you held them firmly, and when have you crossed or moved them? Which of your boundaries are hard, and which are soft? What happens when others push your boundaries? What about when you push them yourself?

Might one of your perceived boundaries become a threshold you're willing to cross?

CYCLE VI WEEK 2 WAXING MOON

PRECOGNITION AND SYNCHRONICITY

Precognitive dreams—dreams that seem to anticipate the future—have been reported throughout history. As you continue to document your dreams, don't be surprised if elements of them reappear upon waking.

Precognition is more likely to manifest as a mundane coincidence than some great prophecy. All the same, document these instances, no matter how silly or inexact they may seem. Did you dream about a turtle, and then you saw the word "turtle" written on a bus? That counts.

Honoring an uncanny coincidence makes space for it, which allows for more of the same to arise. You may be surprised by the opportunities that reveal themselves to you, imbuing your life with a heightened sense of magic and mystery, even strengthening your connection to the bigger forces at play in the cosmos.

Intuition is innate, immediate knowledge about a situation—the so-called gut feeling. It can be informed by data you're not aware you're processing, or it might work in combination with forces both beyond yourself and within. Intuition is a skill that can be strengthened using tools like tarot cards, runes, a pendulum, **I Ching** coins or yarrow stalks, and other divinatory objects. As your intuition develops, you may eventually find you don't need to rely on tools as much and can trust your own inner judgment.

Dreams, too, can offer this kind of insight. Like other forms of divinatory practice, they have the potential to reveal the energies surrounding a situation, predicting how they might move or change in the future. This doesn't mean they show a final, concrete vision; the future is rarely, if ever, set in stone. It's more like looking up at the sky to predict what the weather will be. If you study meteorology, even as an amateur, you'll have a better idea of what signs to look for and how to use the information available. Eventually, with practice, it becomes second nature.

CONSIDER:

Some predictive dreams are literal, while others unfold symbolically. People who use dreams for their predictive potential may pay close attention to numbers when they appear, relating them to experiences in the waking world. For example, there is a long tradition of using numbers that appear in dreams to gamble or play the lottery.

PLAY:

Most divination systems work best if you approach them with open-ended questions, but for the sake of strengthening your intuitive skills, try out some **predictive exercises** this week:

* When your phone rings, guess who's calling before you answer.
* Predict which team is going to win a sports game.
* When the thought of someone pops into your head, reach out to them, tell them you were thinking of them, and see what they have to say.

It's important not to get too caught up in being right. Instead, notice whether a guess feels different from an intuitive insight. With practice, intuition may come more naturally and clearly to you. Know that you'll never achieve 100 percent accuracy—tendencies shift and change, just as a big storm cloud can pass without releasing any rain.

Carl Jung coined the term **synchronicity** to describe meaningful coincidences. It's a magical feeling when it happens: You're thinking of something, and then it appears! Some people explain synchronicity as statistical probability or **confirmation bias** and say it lacks deeper meaning. But what happens when you let yourself believe there's more to it? And if you follow that path—then what *does* cause it?

Even if synchronicity is nothing more than random chance, it's still fun to play with and celebrate. Take it too seriously, though, and it can get overwhelming, or even unhealthy: You might start obsessing over patterns and overanalyzing everything around you. Like most things, it's best to approach synchronicity in moderation—avoid going too far in any one direction.

EXPLORE:

This week, strengthen your intuition by becoming acquainted (or reacquainted) with divination tools. Tarot cards are a good method for any level of experience because they are so visually rich. **Bibliomancy** is another accessible method:

Choose a book, open to a page at random, put your finger down on the page, and read the words you landed on as a message of guidance or response to your query. Flipping coins, either casually for yes/no questions or in the more complex system of I Ching consultation, is another option.

Try out a couple of these methods with an open mind and see what messages you receive.

REFLECT:

Notice whether you have any personal dreaming tendencies—do your dreams tend to be predictive? Are they rich with symbolism? Or are they mostly filled with day residues, punctuated by the occasional wish fulfillment?

How we interpret our dreams can determine what they are and change what they mean—but even still, you might notice that certain types of dreams occur more frequently for you.

CYCLE VI WEEK 3 FULL MOON

BIG DREAMS

We've talked about what Carl Jung calls Big Dreams: the epic, transcendent dreams that leave the dreamer with a sense of awe and mystery upon waking, feeling like they experienced something that came from beyond their own psyche. These types of dreams are what the prophets experienced and recorded in the holy books, but everyday people continue to have Big Dreams, too.

Big Dreams can be an especially powerful resource during times of personal or societal crisis, offering guidance or a sense of purpose. These are the transformative dreams that lead to profound insight and integration.

EXPLORE:

If you've had a Big Dream in the past, spend a few minutes writing it down as a story. Alternatively, record yourself telling it, or share it with someone you trust. Investigate any relevance it may have had to your life and decision-making at the time. Think back on the circumstances surrounding its appearance and consider how the dream may have changed your trajectory.

This sort of dream can give our lives a sense of meaning and direction, shaping our approach to the world around us.

Reflect on these questions in your journal: How did you make sense of your Big Dream at the time? How would you make sense of it now, after these months of dreamwork?

CONJURE:

If you haven't had any Big Dreams and you feel you could use some prophetic guidance at this moment in your life, allow yourself to be open to the idea. Remember that Big Dreams come to us *when they're needed*—often when we're at a crossroads or in conflict—however, by maintaining an open mind and treating our dreams with reverence, we might increase the odds of a powerful message.

To conjure a Big Dream, consider carefully what you're seeking before you ask for it. When you're ready, tell your dream-self that you're willing to receive instruction, affirming this in your journal with a written intention. Keep in mind that this is a request, and it's important to stay humble, perhaps even calling on a dream spirit for support.

Dreams, in your infinite wisdom, please provide me with a message of guidance in my life.

I welcome divine guidance into my dreams.

Dear Spirit, please bring me a dream of transformative wisdom. Bring me courage and help me find my role in this uncertain future.

Remember, while Big Dreams can help on a personal level, their strongest gift is in how they link us to the greater collective, illuminating our purpose within the context of something larger.

FAMOUS DREAMS FROM HISTORY

Dreams have influenced waking reality as we know it countless times, from small-scale personal choices to large-scale societal shifts. Many breakthroughs in philosophy, science, and literature have been catalyzed by dreams.

- **HARRIET TUBMAN** had oracular dreams outlining routes she would use to establish the Underground Railroad, the secret network of safehouses that would lead many enslaved people out of the American South. In 1860, Tubman dreamed vividly of a great storm, followed by a vision of Black people rising up to claim their freedom. She interpreted the dream to mean that the Civil War would bring emancipation—a premonition that brought her such overwhelming joy that she couldn't eat breakfast that morning. When the Emancipation Proclamation was in fact decreed three years later, Tubman remained calm, having already celebrated this momentous event in her dreams.

- **ISAAC FRAUENTHAL** was a lawyer on board the "unsinkable" *Titanic* in 1912. When the ship first struck an iceberg in the North Atlantic, no one was too concerned—except Mr. Frauenthal. Before embarking on the voyage, he'd had a dream that the *Titanic* would crash and sink, so when he heard of the collision, he took the news seriously. He woke his brother, and they jumped into a lifeboat immediately. Of course, the ship did sink, and others weren't so lucky—fifteen hundred people drowned or froze to death in the icy waters.

- **AUGUST KEKULÉ** was a German chemist who was working out the structure of the chemical compound benzene—something scientists of the time were struggling to confirm. One night, he had a dream of an **ouroboros**—a snake eating its own tail. The dream offered a solution to his problem: Benzene's structure was a ring!

DISCERNING ORACLES

Many cultures have classified certain dreams as false, believing they were sent by deities to deceive or confuse humans.

Draumskrok was the Viking term for "false prophecy"—literally "dream nonsense." These were dreams that seemed to predict the future but were nothing more than illusions and gibberish, never destined to come true.

In ancient Greek lore, true dreams were said to pass through gates of horn—"horn" being linked to the word for "fulfill"—while false dreams came through gates of ivory, a cognate with "deceit." Most dreams, it was believed, came through ivory, while only a rare few passed through horn.

In times when dreams were taken seriously—guiding decisions in politics, war, and leadership—false prophecies posed a real danger. Ancient texts often warned against trusting dreams too easily. This is why many societies appointed respected dream interpreters: spiritual figures believed to be divinely chosen and specially trained to discern true prophecy from fraudulence. From a more skeptical view, it's easy to imagine how interpreters might be swayed—consciously or not—by the rewards of telling leaders what they wanted to hear.

REFLECT:

One of the most interesting aspects of Big Dreams is their potential to stretch across time—linking generations past with those yet to come.

Does your family have any lore surrounding dreams? Stories of ancestors who had precognitive or prophetic dreams? If you can, do some digging. Ask around. You might uncover threads of dreaming that may have influenced your family's fate.

CHECK IN:

Spend some time with your dream journal under the full moon this week. Choose a dream and try to interpret it using one of the symbol-interpretation strategies discussed in Cycle V, Week 4. Then try looking at it from other angles. What could it be telling you on a spiritual level? On a psychological level? Could it be prophetic or predictive in some way, or fulfilling some kind of wish? How is this dream a mirror for you?

DREAM INCUBATION

Dream incubation is the practice of planting a seed for what you want to dream about, with the hope that it will bloom into insight or resolution while you sleep. It can be used intentionally—for guidance through dilemmas, as we explore more deeply in Cycle XI, Week 2—or it can be practiced casually. We've already tried this with the "Conjure" prompts: for instance, when you invited the moon into your dreams in Cycle I, Week 3; in the Collaborative Dreaming section at the end of the atlas, you'll find suggestions for taking this skill even further.

Like seeds, not every dream intention will sprout. And just as a seasoned gardener has a better chance of success than a novice, your dream incubation skills may improve over time, with patience, attention, and practice.

The word INCUBATION comes from the Latin *incubare*, meaning "to lie upon," and in the biological sense refers to birds warming their eggs by sitting on them so they hatch. Think of this action—of tenderly sleeping on an idea overnight so it can crack open into a new form.

PLAY:

Incubation can be used to invite a specific person, place, or thing into your dreams. Here's a simple way to begin, by focusing on an animal:

* **Choose your dream subject.** Start small: Pick a specific animal to focus on. Maybe it's a favorite animal of yours or one you know a lot about.
* **Find a representation.** Look for a picture, figurine, or stuffed version of the animal you've chosen.
* **Speak your intention.** As you lie in bed, focus on the image or object and state your wish: *Visit me in my dreams tonight.*
* **Place it with care.** Set the image or object on your dream altar or tuck it under your pillow.

Finally, close your eyes and welcome the animal into your dream space. In the morning, document any encounters in your dream journal.

GO DEEPER

Try calling forth the same animal each night this week, and notice the different ways it materializes.

You might not dream of the animal on your first try, but pay attention to any details that might connect back to the animal: an animal in the same family, a person who resembles the animal, a skill the animal is known for. Count any such details as a step toward success.

CONSIDER:

As you have probably already discovered, dreams don't always obey our wishes, which makes incubation an unpredictable practice. Dreams can respond to requests for answers and advice—but they may not supply the most straightforward reply, or it may not arrive in the timeliest fashion.

With incubation, especially, it's unlikely you'll achieve the desired results on your first night. Be patient, and try not to get discouraged. These skills generally take time and practice to develop. And because dreams tend to be mischievous, the thing you've been trying to dream about might only appear once you've stopped consciously chasing it—sometimes long after you've forgotten about it!

REFLECT:

Take a moment to review and honor any times along your journey when dreams have offered answers to the questions you've asked. Every time you write an intention, you are in fact engaging in incubation—opening a dialogue with the dreaming world.

Tonight, speak your gratitude aloud. Like any friend, your dreams might appreciate being acknowledged.

DREAMING JOURNEY:
ASIA

CHINA
EARLY FOUNDATIONS: THE DUKE OF ZHOU

The earliest known Chinese dream interpreter was Ji Dan, also known as the **Duke of Zhou**—a revered statesman and philosopher from the early Zhou dynasty who was later associated with the Ming dynasty through adaptations of his work. He is credited with the classic text *The Interpretation of Dreams*, which has been rewritten and expanded several times over the centuries.

The Duke of Zhou's dream book introduced a classification system dividing dreams into six categories:

* **Zheng-meng** ~ Ordinary dreams with no deeper meaning
* **E-meng** ~ Nightmares, believed to result from immoral behavior
* **Si-meng** ~ Dreams of yearning, shaped by obsession or desire
* **Wu-meng** ~ Transient dreams (hypnagogic dreams)
* **Xi-meng** ~ Happy dreams, born of joy
* **Qu-meng** ~ Anxiety dreams, born of waking fears

Later additions included:

* **Gan-meng** ~ Dreams influenced by weather or the environment (e.g., dreary weather will cause a depressing dream)
* **Shi-meng** ~ Dreams shaped by the seasons (e.g., autumn dreams focus on harvest and preparation; winter dreams are introspective; spring dreams focus on growth and emergence; summer dreams are boundless and free)

Some of the symbols in the Duke of Zhou's writings have different meanings than in Western tradition—for example, snakes in Zhou's *Interpretation of Dreams* represent wisdom, whereas in Western tradition they often represent danger or untrustworthiness. It's an important reminder that symbols are culturally specific and ought to be interpreted in context.

TAOISM

By the third century BCE, **Taoism** had emerged as a major spiritual philosophy in China. In Taoist thought, dreaming is seen as a path to spiritual freedom—a release from the attachments and distractions of waking life. Waking from a dream is likened to awakening from illusion, a metaphor for enlightenment.

*One night, Taoist philosopher **Zhuang-Zhou** dreamt he was a carefree butterfly. He fluttered from flower to flower, tasting nectar and enjoying the blue skies and sunlight on his wings. When Zhuang-Zhou woke up, he mused: "Am I a philosopher who dreamed he was a butterfly? Or am I a butterfly who is now dreaming he is a human philosopher?"*

HUN-PO: THE SOUL'S NIGHTLY JOURNEY

In Chinese tradition, there are two aspects of the soul: ***hun*** 魂, the spiritual, and ***po*** 魄, the physical. During sleep, the hun (spirit) is said to leave the po (body) and travel to the realm of dreaming. Along its journey, the hun might visit the land of the dead—another example of the connection between dreaming and death we see in many cultures. However, if the dreamer is awakened too suddenly, the hun might not make it back to the po in time, and the soul will end up separated from its body. The hun might also enter another's body; there are tales of dreamers' spirits entering the bodies of animals or other humans, sometimes becoming trapped, leaving their original bodies paralyzed or empty.

QI: DREAMS AS DIAGNOSIS

According to traditional Chinese medicine, dreams are tied to the flow of **qi**—the essential life force that animates all beings. **Yin** and **yang**—two manifestations of qi—are complementary energies of shadow and light, receptivity and action. Neither can exist without the other, and unity is achieved through balance. Dreams are a space where these seemingly opposite energies can exist simultaneously. Dreams can also be used as diagnostic tools, revealing imbalances in the body or spirit. A troubling dream might signal a disruption in qi, offering insight into how to restore harmony and health.

JAPAN

In Japanese culture, the playful nature of dreams—especially their reliance on puns and wordplay—is celebrated. Certain objects are auspicious because the words for them are homophones for other good things, thus dreaming of them foretells good fortune. **Hatsuyume**, the first dream of the new year, is especially important, as it's said to forecast what the rest of the year will be like. To increase the odds of dreaming of specific omens on the eve of the new year, many people place a picture under their pillow of the Seven Lucky Gods—a group of seven deities, each with their own domain—traveling together in a treasure-laden ship.

LUCKY DREAM SYMBOLS IN JAPANESE CULTURE:

- **Mount Fuji:** Its name sounds like the word for "immortality," and its towering peak symbolizes greatness and achievement.
- **Hawk:** The word sounds similar to "higher," and the hawk is an intelligent, majestic bird.
- **Eggplant:** The word sounds like "to accomplish" or "to achieve."
- **Fan:** Historically, wealthy landowners flapped paper fans to signal agreement, so fans have come to signify affirmation, or "yes."
- **Tobacco smoke:** Like Mount Fuji, smoke rises to great heights.
- **Bald man:** The Japanese word resembles the phrase for "injury-free," making it a symbol of safety and protection.

If a person tries to conjure these images and fails, they can throw the drawing of the Seven Lucky Gods into a river or another body of water, symbolically letting go of misfortune. And if things really turn ugly, they can always enlist the services of the **Baku**—the dream-eating spirit! (See page 165.)

INDONESIA

Dreaming is a primary source of spirituality for the **Iban** people of Indonesia. They believe in a constant flow back and forth between the waking world and the dreaming realm—two distinct yet interconnected realities. While they recognize the difference between the two, the experiences of the soul during dreams are considered real and meaningful.

After death, the spirit is believed to continue its existence in the dreamworld, where it can still communicate with the living. This connection is celebrated in a sacred event known as **gawai mimpi**, or the "dream festival," during which individuals receive dreams from ancestors and deities. Dreams determine when the ceremony should take place and which offerings need to be readied.

KOREA

In Korean tradition, good-luck dreams can be bought and sold. If someone has a particularly fortunate dream, they may choose to keep it secret, because sharing it is thought to diminish its power. However, there's another option: One can sell the dream, transferring its potency and luck to the buyer by sharing its details. This kind of transaction is mostly done between close friends and family, since the system relies on trust—after all, there's no way to prove a dream occurred.

In Korean dream symbolism, the most desirable dreams are ones involving pigs, as pigs symbolize wealth and prosperity.

CYCLE VII

DREAMS AND ART

CYCLE VII WEEK 1 ◯ NEW MOON

DREAMS AND CREATIVITY

Countless creative people throughout history have looked to dreams to inspire their work—not only visual artists but also filmmakers, musicians, composers, writers, architects, and others. Dreaming and creation are both acts that engage abstract thinking, symbolism, and spontaneity. Thus, dreaming can inspire art, and art can help an individual interpret and process dreams.

CONSIDER:

All humans are born with an innate need and ability to creatively express themselves through art, movement, words, and more. You don't have to be a professional artist to benefit from the exercises in this cycle, but if you are, they can support your practice. Either way, what you create during this time is not intended to be judged on merit or skill. You're not trying to produce finished pieces for critique; the primary objective is to rejuvenate your creative mindset.

It is the artists who dream for society.

—Meret Oppenheim

THE SURREALISTS

The **Surrealists** were a group of artists who drew inspiration from dreams, believing in the revolutionary power of the imagination to reshape society. In 1924, in postwar France, writer **André Breton**—who had served during World War I in a psychiatric hospital, where he encountered Freudian psychoanalysis used to treat soldiers experiencing shell shock—published the *Surrealist Manifesto*, formally launching the movement. Many other artists around Europe joined Breton, creating work that tapped into the collective unconscious as a source of liberation, creativity, and social change.

As political tensions escalated in Europe in the lead-up to World War II, Surrealist artists were increasingly persecuted, their influential work considered a threat to the fascist ideologies gaining power. Some paid the ultimate price: Surrealist painter **Felix Nussbaum** was murdered along with his family at Auschwitz. Others, like artist **Meret Oppenheim**, fled to Switzerland, where she suffered an eighteen-year depression. Many other Surrealists went into exile, clustering in pockets of North and South America, where they continued using their dreams and art to process the trauma of war and displacement.

EXPLORE:

Although Surrealists are well-known for their explicit dream advocacy, they are by no means the only artists to channel the mystical qualities of our sleeping realm. **Symbolism** and **Romanticism** were two earlier art movements that pulled from the ethereal world of dreams. And much like Freud and Jung, the Surrealists were heavily inspired by dream-influenced folk art from around the world. For as long as art has existed, artists have looked to their dreams—whether to reproduce the experience of dreaming itself or to draw inspiration from their visions.

Go to the library and check out some art books or exhibition catalogs of artists who have been directly inspired by dreams. The Surrealists are a good place to start, but feel free to do your own research and seek out artists who speak to you. Look closely at the images. Notice whether any resemble your own dream landscapes. What feelings do these artworks evoke? Do they raise any questions for you? How do these unusual images provoke a shift in thinking?

GO DEEPER

Visit a gallery or an art museum to get a closer look at dream-influenced art up close and in person.

PLAY:

This week, instead of (or in addition to) recording your dream when you wake, move your pen freely along your journal page, allowing lines and shapes to appear intuitively. Don't attempt to illustrate your dream—just move your hand and see what happens.

When you're finished, take a look at your drawing. Do any images, shapes, or designs repeat themselves? Ask yourself where these shapes or patterns might come from and what they might represent on a deeper level.

This method of creation is sometimes called **automatic drawing** (or **automatic writing**, when words are involved), and it was a popular technique employed by Surrealist artists. The idea is that by giving the rational, analytical mind a rest, the unexpected has an opportunity to emerge—offering revelation in much the same way that dreams do.

CONJURE:

Choose a piece of art that appeals to you and meditate on it before bed. If this artwork exists in your home, stand before it for a few minutes as though you were visiting it in a museum. Otherwise, look at the piece online or in a book. As you take in the work, see if new details emerge. Set an intention to enter its landscape in your dreams, exploring its terrain while you sleep.

CHECK IN:

Have you been keeping up with writing down your dreams? It's especially useful during this cycle and the next to continue recording your dreams so you have plenty of material to draw from in your artistic practice. If you've been letting it slide, just open your journal to the next blank page tonight and write a quick "hello!" to your dream-self. Then, come morning, write a couple of notes about what you experienced in your sleep—even if it's just "slept soundly; can't recall a dream."

CYCLE VII WEEK 2 WAXING MOON

EXPLORING COLOR

Much of our waking life is spent in the world of words: thinking, talking, writing emails and texts, having conversations, describing things, searching for the right word . . . how exhausting! Verbal communication helps us find mutual understanding, and words can give ideas form—but existence and experience can live beyond words, too.

*Philosophers such as **Ludwig Wittgenstein** used the concept of color to illustrate subjectivity: While we all use terms like "blue" and "red," there's no way to prove that we share the same visual experience of them—the words themselves are an agreement.*

Focusing on color this week, both out in the world and in your dreams, may be a welcome break from putting things into words. Colors are attached to symbolism, but even by themselves, they evoke unique qualities and moods. Thinking in color is an intuitive, primal way of processing things. Notice how it can bring a sense of quiet to your mind.

EXPLORE:

Begin experimenting with color, inviting it into your awareness and engaging with it more intentionally:

* **Saturate.** Gather some art supplies—oil pastels, crayons, markers, or paint—and make some bold marks. Fill an entire page with color.
* **Mix and match.** Pick up some paint strips from a hardware store; cut them up and shuffle them around, noticing how they influence each other and how different combinations change your perception of them.
* **Visualize.** Before bed, focus on a single color that appeals to you. Then, when you close your eyes, see if you can summon that color. Does anything else surface along with the color—a feeling, texture, or movement? Can you make different colors appear behind your eyes? Does *green* have a different personality than *pink*?

GO DEEPER

Settle on one color, perhaps thinking of it as a living entity, and try to travel into sleep with it; see if you can call it into your dreams. Maybe it appears as a personality, or maybe it's more of a tint that infuses everything with some of its energy.

REFLECT:

Return to your dream journal and look for any times you've mentioned colors. Consider whether the colors have any kind of symbolic resonance based on their context.

As you continue to flip through your old entries, think about what color you'd assign any given dream. Don't overthink it—is that a brown dream? A yellow dream? A pink and turquoise dream?

If you enjoy doing this, assign all your dreams a color! When you're finished, go back and see which dreams belong to the same color family. You might be surprised by the connections this reveals.

CONSIDER:

Prior to the twentieth century, written accounts of dreams often contained colors. Once photography became commonplace, however, more people remembered their dreams in black and white—like the photos, newspapers, and films they saw. A study from 1942 recorded that about 70 percent of people said they dreamed only in black and white. But once color film and photography became mainstream after the 1950s, this ratio reversed again, with the majority of people reporting dreaming in color.

How else might movies and media influence how we visualize and narrate our dreams?

CYCLE VII WEEK 3 FULL MOON

CONTEXT AND JUXTAPOSITION

What something means depends largely on its **context**—its environment and what surrounds it. What does a million dollars mean to a man dying of thirst? What does a cat mean to a mouse, and what does it mean to a child? The same object can carry vastly different meanings depending on the situation.

Juxtaposition is the act of placing things side by side to highlight contrast. Sometimes this contrast creates surprise; other times, the combination is unexpectedly harmonious. Dreams are full of odd juxtaposition—images and ideas that don't logically belong together, yet somehow make sense. Artists, especially the Surrealists, treasured this technique, using it to unlock new ways of seeing and feeling.

PLAY:

This week, gather a collection of knickknacks, stones, shells, bottle caps, tchotchkes, and other random objects. Create a small dream assemblage on your bedside table, perhaps incorporating it into your dream altar. Alternatively, arrange your objects inside a cigar box or shoebox. Stack your objects, move them around, suspend them—play with their placement and combination.

GO DEEPER

Using the same collection of items, create a new tableau each night this week before falling asleep. See if the different arrangements influence your dreaming. If you'd like, think of this activity as a dream ritual.

EXPLORE:

Read through your dream journal with an eye for visually evocative phrases and circle those that stand out to you. On a blank piece of paper, rewrite what you've circled, each phrase on its own line. Next, cut out the phrases. Rearrange your scraps and combine them in different pairings and groups. Move them around again and see how they change depending on their context and position.

Next, gather scissors, glue, and some magazines you don't mind cutting up—you're going to make an old-school collage. Flip through the magazines and cut out any images that catch your fancy. Follow the edges of the shapes as you cut, letting your intuition guide you.

Once you've collected a few images, begin to move them around. Try placing them against different backgrounds and notice how the story shifts: What changes when the woman on the phone is standing in the desert instead of a grocery store? What happens if she's next to a baby, or a cake, or a tiger?

GO DEEPER

Combine your strips of words with the magazine images to create a mixed-media collage. If a particular arrangement of words and images resonates with you, you can glue it into your dream journal. Otherwise, store your loose clippings and dream strips in an envelope or folder. Before bed, you can revisit them, rearranging the pieces as a meditative exercise.

REFLECT:

This is once again the week of the full moon, and we're at the midpoint in this year of dreamwork. Celebrate the moment by finding ways to incorporate art into your monthly full-moon dream ritual. Here are a few possibilities:

* Invite a friend to make some art with you. Put on some music, get out some paint, and let your dreams of the past month guide you. Collaborate on a piece together or work side-by-side on individual pieces.
* Share your work with loved ones, showing it to them and telling them about it, or giving it to them as a present.
* Hang your creations on or near your bedside altar.
* Display your art somewhere publicly—perhaps leave it as an offering in a park or at a bus stop.
* Make art for, rather than about, your dreams.

CONSIDER:

Often, when we wake from a dream, what remains feels incomplete—vague, disjointed shards of feeling or image. The larger story slips away, leaving only a trace. We were just there, but now we can't remember where there *was.*

Rather than trying in vain to remember what's vanished, embrace what lingers. Celebrate the fragments: the jagged edges, the shifting fog, the desire and nostalgia they evoke. Your dream journal may be filled with half-formed phrases and unresolved moments—more questions than answers. Think of these fragments as archaeological artifacts: though incomplete, they are beautiful precisely because they've survived the crossing of the dream-veil.

The **Dada movement**, a precursor to Surrealism, emerged in response to the senseless violence and destruction of World War I. In protest, Dada artists embraced randomness and absurdity, creating works that defied logic and traditional aesthetics. Among their signature techniques were visual and verbal collages and **assemblages**—sculptural compositions made from found objects.

One artist known for his surreal assemblages, though not technically a Dadaist or even a Surrealist, was **Joseph Cornell**. Living quietly in New York with his mother and brother, Cornell spent his free time walking the streets of New York, visiting antique stores and collecting discarded objects. He assembled these fragments into shadow boxes: three-dimensional collages that evoked a dreamlike sense of wonder—the nostalgia of ***eterniday***, as he named it.

ILLUSTRATION

Prior to this cycle, we explored dream interpretation as a way of connecting dreams to waking life—uncovering the deeper meanings they might communicate. But "interpretation" can also mean reimagining something from a new point of view—**interpretive dance**, for example, is a way of expressing emotion through movement. By translating our dreams into a different medium, we might discover meanings that words alone can't express.

This week, the goal is not to create a polished masterpiece. Rather, this is an invitation to step away from critical thinking and let your intuition guide you. Frame your art-making practice as an effort to externalize your dream—giving it shape and presence in the waking world. The result becomes a kind of amulet, a physical object that holds the power of your subconscious.

When you turn ephemeral dream images into art, you give them form and weight; you make the invisible material. And while doing so, you might find yourself entering a dreamlike state even when awake—one that is both restorative and revealing.

REFLECT:

Review the entries in your dream journal and look for any particularly potent images. Try your hand at sketching these written descriptions. Even if you're unsure of your artistic skills, give it a try.

Later, look over your illustrations or show them to someone else. Ask yourself or your friend what the image might mean or symbolize: What feelings does the image evoke? What ideas does it suggest?

Next, try depicting a whole dream as a comic strip or drawing. Focus on one particular dream or combine elements from different dreams to produce a sort of narrative collage. How can you represent the layered, dynamic nature of a dream on a one-dimensional surface?

EXPLORE:

If the very thought of drawing or painting stresses you out, try working with modeling clay instead, roughly sculpting the images, symbols, or feelings you find in your dream journal. You can also channel the ancient Mesopotamians, rolling the clay into a ball, pressing it flat like a stone tablet, and using a toothpick to carve words or images from your dreams onto the surface. Perhaps you want to try interpreting your dreams using movement or music. Reread a dream in your journal, copy it down, and then—keeping the dream in mind as a source of inspiration—improvise a dance or tinker away with a musical instrument.

PLAY:

You can also use paint to give form to your dreams in the waking world. Watercolor, in particular, is a looser medium, easier to blend and morph, so it may feel more natural to use when trying to express the protean dream landscape.

Try laying down some blobs of color. Wait for them to dry, then use a fine-line pen to draw images from your dreams over the painted background.

HINT: *Summon a dreamlike mindset to your art-making practice by infusing it with elements of your full-moon sleep ritual—light a candle, press "Play" on your favorite dreamy playlist, dim the lights, spritz your dream spray in the air, and get to work!*

William Blake (1757–1827) was a poet, painter, and printmaker whose dreams and mystical visions inspired his work. At the age of eight, he had a vision of a tree filled with angels. Throughout his youth he continued to have remarkable experiences, and he would retreat into his vivid imagination to escape his rigid upbringing. As he grew older, he combined handwritten text with ink drawings to illustrate his visions. Even his technique was inspired by his dreams:

He was visited in a dream by his beloved dead brother, Robert, who showed him a new method of printmaking that heavily influenced his illustrated masterpiece *Songs of Innocence*. Blake believed in the power of dreams to liberate the imagination and bring forth truth, wisdom, and vision.

DREAMING JOURNEY:
AFRICA

ANCESTRAL COMMUNION

In most African cultures, there is a strong link between ancestors and dreaming. Ancestors are honored and revered long after they've passed on—but they are distinguished from gods, who are far more powerful, primordial, and worshipped. Ancestors are seen as a bridge between the earthly and the divine, and because of this position, they are regarded positively as intercessors. They are often seen as protectors of the living, and the living in turn owe them deep respect.

A particularly revered type of dream in these cultures is the **visitation dream**. In it, a departed loved one appears to the dreamer, not as a symbolic figure or a product of grief but as the actual spirit of the deceased. These dreams are understood as genuine encounters with the immortal soul, which continues to exist even after the physical body expires. Dreaming thus becomes an effective way to maintain a relationship and communicate with beloved family members who have passed on.

Ancestral spirits may also use dreams to deliver essential information to the living: messages, warnings, or guidance. However, dreamers must avoid physical contact with spirits during these encounters. It's primarily the newly departed who attempt to touch the living; in their confused state, they might try to draw the living with them into the realm of the dead.

SPIRIT SPOUSES

In Cote d'Ivoire, on the west coast of Africa, it is said that everyone has a **spirit spouse**—a spiritual partner, usually very beautiful in appearance, who is paired with them before birth. These spirit spouses are honored with carved wooden statues and personal shrines, but when a spirit spouse becomes angry or jealous, they can cause stress in a person's life. In such cases, people may consult spiritual authorities to help in understanding and resolving the conflict, restoring harmony between the human and their otherworldly partner.

KINSHIP

Among the **Yansi** people of Central Africa, dreams are shared only with highly trusted individuals, such as friends, family, and spiritual leaders; it's considered risky to share something so intimate as a dream with anyone else. Those trusted individuals will help analyze dreams, looking for warnings and other kinds of valuable insight. If the dream requires additional analysis, it's brought to a professional .dream diviner to interpret.

DIVINERS

In some African cultures, diviners are well respected, offering spiritual guidance and dream interpretation to the rest of the society. Their position is considered a vocation and often begins in childhood with intense, vivid dreams. As the future diviner matures, they are taught to nurture their skills and access deeper dream wisdom through the mentorship of an elder. In addition to interpreting dreams, diviners can dream on behalf of others, acting as intermediaries between the human realm and the spiritual world.

* Among the **Yoruba** people of Nigeria, individuals may seek out the services of a diviner who casts shells and interprets the way they land to gain insight into a situation.
* For the **Xhosa** people of South Africa, visiting a diviner may involve a ritual that includes **ubulawu**—a frothy herbal infusion made by grinding specific roots. Those seeking guidance imbibe the mixture, which causes them to vomit: a purging or purification. Following the ritual, the seeker experiences vivid and often prophetic dreams. While anyone can undergo ubulawu, it is a significant spiritual experience that is believed to sometimes enable direct contact with ancestors. Xhosa diviners themselves use it regularly to deepen their exploration of the spiritual realms.

TYPES OF DREAMS

As we've seen in other traditions, many African cultures draw distinctions between different types of dreams. For example, in the Yansi language**, *ndoey mutwe*** are "dreams of the head," the trivial, day-to-day dreams, while ***ndoey ndeag*** are divine, prophetic dreams. In Swahili, ***mawazo*** are holy dreams, or seeds of divine thought.

Before we were created, we humans first existed as mawazo in the mind of God.

KN

CYCLE VIII

DREAMS AND WRITING

CYCLE VIII WEEK 1

NEW MOON

DREAMING IN VERSE

Dreams and poetry often share the same language. The two can inform and invigorate each other, especially when there's a conscious flow between them. Many poets are aware of this exchange, with countless works inspired by—or documenting—the dream realm.

*Symbolist poet **Saint-Pol-Roux** kept a sign on his bedroom door while he slept that said, "Poet at Work."*

EXPLORE:

If you visit the Poetry Foundation website and type "dream" into the search bar, you'll find hundreds of dreams published as poems by celebrated authors of diverse backgrounds. Reading, in general, is a great way to ease yourself into sleep, but it's best not to look at screens right before bed, so print out a few poems or keep a collection of poetry on your nightstand. Over the course of this week, try to read a poem each night before going to sleep.

It's said that reading helps a person fall asleep because the movement of the eyes back and forth across the page mimics the soothing sway of a rocking cradle. If you were read to as a child, your brain might also associate reading with falling asleep.

PLAY:

Find a poem by another poet that speaks to you and write it in your dream journal. Read the poem each night this week before bed—silently to yourself, or aloud—perhaps even memorizing it. Envision carrying the words with you into sleep, like a talisman or charm.

Aimé and Suzanne Césaire were Black poets from the Caribbean island of Martinique, then under French colonial rule. Together, they helped found the **Négritude** movement in the 1940s—a branch of Surrealism that took inspiration from the Harlem Renaissance and focused on anticolonialism. For Aimé Césaire, Surrealism was a way to dive deep into the subconscious and connect with his African ancestors. Suzanne Césaire saw it as more than an art movement: To her, it was a state of mind—a "permanent readiness for the Marvelous." Both believed Surrealism could strengthen revolution rather than distract from it. As Suzanne wrote, it "nourishes an impatient strength within us, endlessly reinforcing the massive army of refusals."

REFLECT:

Sift through your dreams once again, referring to your journal or your typed transcriptions. If it's been a while since you've rewritten some of your dreams, this would be a good time to do so! You don't have to type them all up, but choose a few favorites to spend some extra time with. Print one out or open it in your laptop, reworking it using one or more of these methods:

* **Recast.** Break up lines, cross out words, and rearrange them. Play around with punctuation and the way the words fall on the page. Let your dream entries take a new shape, and see how that changes the impact of the text. You can even try playing with font style and size.
* **Impose limits.** Try turning a dream into a structured poem, such as a haiku, a sonnet, a rhyming couplet, or a limerick. Although a poem doesn't have to rhyme or follow a specific framework, sometimes rules and parameters offer inspiration, and some poets find forms or limitations to be helpful. Notice how the rigid form of certain types of poetry offers contrast to the fluidity of dreams.

***Prose poetry** is a type of poetry without line breaks that offers a poignant snapshot in just a few sentences or paragraphs. As with other poetic forms, every word in a prose poem is considered for how it contributes to the piece as a whole.*

* **Lyricize.** Review your dreams and search for recurring themes, objects, colors, people, or places. Ruminate on these elements and use them as a springboard for a poem. For example, if the ocean has appeared in more than one dream, write a short poem about the sea.
* **Flow.** If a certain thought, image, or phrase appeals to you, try elaborating on it in your journal. Follow the phrase like it's a river, seeing where it leads. Silence your inner editor for now (the part of your brain that tries to discern, clarify, and improve), and see what happens when you let yourself drift down the unusual streams of your dream consciousness.

You can also put your dream journal aside and work from memory or imagination.

* **Invent.** Make up a dream. Spontaneously combine imagery, symbols, and descriptive language to create a dreamlike atmosphere and imaginary dreamworld. After all, artmaking can be a form of dreaming while awake.
* **Remember.** Describe a dream you remember having—it can be a dream from childhood, one of your more memorable dreams, or one you had recently.

CYCLE VIII WEEK 2 

WAXING MOON

LITERARY DREAMS

Dreams are a narrative device that can be found peppered throughout all kinds of storytelling—used to advance storylines, reveal secret depths, add layers of symbolism, and sometimes, when the **deus ex machina** cliché is employed, neatly resolve improbable plot holes: *"It was all just a dream!"*

Have you recently encountered a dream in a book or film? How was it used to tell the story?

Like characters from literature, many writers have received dreams that sparked some of their most imaginative and enduring stories.

- Author **John Steinbeck** referred to his dreams as the "committee of sleep"—a trusted source he turned to when stuck on tricky plot points or battling writer's block.
- **Mary Shelley** was just nineteen when she joined a group of writers vacationing at their friend Lord Byron's estate. Over dinner, a challenge was announced to see who could write the most frightening horror story. That night, Mary dreamed about a doctor who stitched together a man from cadaver parts and brought him to life. That dream became *Frankenstein*—now one of the most iconic horror stories of all time.
- **Robert Louis Stevenson** also found inspiration in sleep. He literally dreamed up *The Strange Case of Dr. Jekyll and Mr. Hyde*, another chilling tale that explores the dark, hidden sides of human nature. The story reminds us that the fears we refuse to face can end up controlling us, even as we go to great lengths to avoid them.
- On a lighter note, **E. B. White** had a dream about a little talking mouse dressed in human clothes. When he woke up, he jotted down the idea, and it eventually became *Stuart Little*, a classic of children's literature.

EXPLORE:

Several famous authors have published their dream journals.

- **Graham Greene** kept one from 1965 until 1989, ultimately amassing over eight hundred pages of material. Every night before bed, Greene would reread his work from that day, hoping to dream through creative blockages—and sometimes, to dream through his characters' eyes. Near the end of his life, he selected highlights from his journals for a book titled *A World of My Own: A Dream Diary*, which was published posthumously in 1992.
- **Jack Kerouac** described his *Book of Dreams* as an "autobiography of the soul," a dreamlike counterpart to his famous novel *On the Road*.

* The extensive diaries of **Franz Kafka** are a chaotic assortment of story ideas, self-analysis, masochistic fantasies, and dreams. By day, he worked as an insurance official; by night, he battled insomnia and wrote feverishly. Many of his most haunting stories emerged from this liminal, sleep-deprived state.

If nothing else, these references illustrate the merits of keeping a dream journal. Look for any published dream journals at your local library or bookshop, and notice what it feels like to inhabit someone else's dreamscape for a time.

REFLECT:

Before bed this week, in lieu of writing an intention in your journal, review your day and choose a poetic moment, image, or scene you witnessed or experienced, then describe it in a few words or lines. Later, when you wake up from dreaming, follow this day entry with a brief dream entry—creating a poetic call-and-response form of journaling.

After a few nights of this experiment, read over your day and night reflections, noting how these snippets are in dialogue with one another.

CHECK IN:

As we've charted through a few months of dreamwork, you've likely adapted your intention on some nights to suit specific situations. Remember that the core intention you began with—some version of, *I will dream, and I will remember my dream when I wake up*—is always available to you. Return to it anytime you feel out at sea.

PLAY:

Ideas are funny things with lives of their own. Though dreams can be a wellspring of inspiration, it requires discipline to record them and even more effort to develop them into something polished and complete.

Pick one of your dreams and read it over. Then, use one of the prompts below to develop it into a short piece of fiction. Write the story beginning to end, seeing where it takes you; then edit your work for clarity, trying to evoke particular emotions or themes. Don't worry if the original dream falls away or is changed beyond recognition.

BEFORE

Imagine what happened before the opening scene of your dream. What happened five minutes ago? Five years ago? Five hundred years ago? Write down your musings, filling in details of setting, character, theme, and motivation.

AFTER

Imagine, if your dream were to continue, what would happen next. Experiment with the linearity of the narrative; dreams don't follow the same cause-and-effect rules of waking reality, and your story doesn't have to, either. Write its natural continuation first, then try taking it in an unexpected direction.

CONFLICT

Does your dream feature a clear conflict? What elements can you add to raise the stakes and heighten the drama? The bigger the risk, the bigger the reward. What happens when you up the ante?

CYCLE VIII WEEK 3 FULL MOON

THE ART OF THE MANIFESTO

Many big thinkers have used the **manifesto**, a public declaration of beliefs, to pin down and share their ambitions and to hold themselves accountable to their philosophies. Manifestos are famously issued by political organizations, but artist movements also use the form—sometimes ironically, sometimes sincerely—to announce their intentions and to attract support. The overlap is no coincidence, as political and artistic spheres often influence and inform one another, the tensions between them shaping the philosophies of an age.

Many artistic manifestos are subversive in nature, rebelling against the status quo and offering alternative visions. The anarchic Dadaists, and later the Surrealists, toyed with the rigid structure of the manifesto to make up and proclaim their own rules.

EXPLORE:

This week, write your own dream manifesto. It may help to read some historical manifestos first.

* **Hugo Ball's** original "Dada Manifesto" of 1916 leans into the nonsensical, while **Tristan Tzara's** 1918 response to Ball—also titled "Dada Manifesto"—pushes absurdity to a point of nihilism.
* The *Surrealist Manifesto*, published by **André Breton** in 1924, defines terms and explores the influences behind the Surrealist movement.
* In 1984, **Peter Schumann** of the **Bread and Puppet Theater** produced a short letterpress manifesto titled "Why Cheap Art?" In it, he spells out simple provisions in a playful and inspiring way, urging everyday people to make, share, and enjoy art with one another.
* "The Afrosurreal Manifesto," written by **D. Scot Miller** in 2009, defines **Afro-Surrealism** as an artistic and cultural movement that reveals the mystical and invisible dimensions of Black reality. Centering the contributions of Black thinkers and creators, it calls for transformation and liberation through the elevation of marginalized voices.

Play around with the absurd and the surreal, or take the form seriously; it's up to you. You can use symbols; you can be abstract; you can be literal. You can be concise or rambling. Use this exercise as an opportunity to examine your values, beliefs, and intentions.

Questions you may want to address in your dream manifesto:

* *Why do you value dreams?*
* *What have you accessed, or what do you hope to access, through your dreams?*
* *What does dreaming mean to you?*
* *What do you bring to dreaming?*

We've explored these questions before, but this is an opportunity to delve into your experiences in a different way.

REFLECT:

After you've written your manifesto, compare it to your dream-self interview from Cycle 1, Week 4. How have your views and understanding of dreams changed over the course of your work so far?

PLAY:

Manifestos are a way of broadcasting your dreams and beliefs. How else might you share yourself with others—and how can you open yourself to accepting what others have to share with you?

- Write some of your favorite or most interesting dreams on index cards, creating a small collection you can shuffle and play with. Choose a card at random and offer it to a friend—or even a stranger, if you're feeling adventurous.
- Organize your dreams by theme and illustrate them: a collection of love dreams, water dreams, animal dreams, or nightmares, for example.
- Collect your dreams in a **zine**—a small, self-published magazine—by folding a few pieces of paper into a chapbook and rewriting your entries on its pages. Make copies and share them with others.

CONJURE:

Have you seen words or writing in your dreams before? Because language and writing mostly activate the left side of the brain, toward the back, and dreaming activates the right side, toward the front, it can be difficult to read in dreams. However, it is possible, especially if you spend a lot of time reading in your waking life. So, if you're up for a challenge, ask your dreams to deliver a written message, and see what they bring you!

CYCLE VIII WEEK 4 WANING MOON

ACTIVE IMAGINATION

Active imagination, a term and practice developed by Carl Jung, is a way of creating a bridge between the conscious mind and the subconscious. Jung described it as a form of spiritual **alchemy**—a process of deep transformation that could lead to understanding and accepting one's full self. He explored the idea in his work *The Red Book,* which he began as a personal diary in 1913, when Europe was on the brink of war and Jung himself was on the verge of a mental breakdown, experiencing daily apocalyptic visions. Determined to regain control of his mind, Jung wrote down and illustrated his experiences, transforming them into something he could more easily face. Entering a hypnagogic state, Jung approached his dreams as an observer, allowing whatever rose to the surface of his mind to act itself out. Afterward, he meticulously recorded everything that unfolded.

Mystic trance is another way of disconnecting from the ego and bridging mental states, practiced through the ages all over the world. Like dreaming, trance opens the mind to different ways of existing and can allow access to unexpected insight.

There are many ways to invoke trance: breathing exercises, chanting, fasting, sleep deprivation, drumming, dancing, and more. Even staring into the embers of a fire or watching the movement of water can be hypnotic, lulling the mind into release.

EXPLORE:

All forms of trance lead to a slackening of connection to one's sense of individuality, evoking an experience not unlike a waking dream. Sometimes this means feeling a profound sense of unity and belonging, of ecstatic oneness and flow with the universe.

Allow your mind to shift away from active thought using one of the following techniques. Try to let go of your ego and let your mind wander.

- **Look up.** Step into nature, even if it's just your yard or a public park. Lie on the ground and gaze at the clouds or tree canopy, focusing on your breath and the movement of these larger bodies above you.
- **Light a candle or incense.** Watch the flame or smoke spiral, allowing your eyes to shift out of focus.
- **Channel a rhythm.** Turn off the lights and play a recording of steady drumming or another form of repetitive music. Let it wash over you and take you into a different state of mind.

Afterward, try to extend this state. Grab a pen and start **freewriting** in your journal: Keep your hand moving on the page until you fill it, front and back. What you write doesn't matter; don't go back to read or edit until you're finished.

If it's helpful to have a prompt, begin with the phrase "*In my dreams...*" and continue the thought. Every time you find yourself coming out of the flow of writing, copy the phrase again, beginning a new line.

HINT: *Later, reflect on what your writing experience was like. Were you recording words that you* ***heard****? Describing things you* ***saw*** *in your mind's eye? Or was it something else?*

Trance can also spotlight division within oneself or create a sense of unreality. Like active imagination, it should be practiced with care. Spiritually ground yourself before attempting to enter a trance, calling on any guides or ancestors you work with to protect you. Alternatively, hold a small stone in your hand that you can squeeze and return to if you feel yourself drifting further than you'd like.

PLAY:

Daydreaming—a more casual version of Jung's active imagination practice—is considered a state of ordinary trance. Other names for this activity are fantasy, reverie, or woolgathering—the latter term originating from the act of idly collecting stray strands of sheep's wool from bushes.

If you're a natural daydreamer, you might have been reprimanded in school and asked to focus on your lessons. Let go of those admonishments, and in the comfort of your home, allow your mind to wander as it pleases, visualizing your goals or picturing things you enjoy. Perhaps you can imagine a beautiful, relaxing place or a satisfying event, bringing it to life by exploring its details in your mind.

After experimenting with gentle reverie for ten minutes or so, use the dreamy energy you've conjured to write. Call on your dreams to guide your hand and see where they lead you. You may think of it as a form of the free association we played with on page 58, following whatever streams your mind takes you down—this time, following memories and fantasies instead of words.

DREAMING JOURNEY:
THE AMERICAS

NORTH AMERICA
VISION QUEST

To the **Ojibwe** people of Canada and the midwestern United States, **inkonze** refers to dreams that bring epiphanies, often through animal visitations that offer valuable information. Animals are thought to have personhood equal to humans and tend to share insights with those who are connected to and work reciprocally with the environment. The inkonze dreams are important gifts: They can provide weather predictions or indicate where to find abundant food. They also play a significant role in coming-of-age rituals.

Among the Ojibwe and other societies, it's traditionally considered unwise to share good dreams, as it is believed to diminish their likelihood of coming true. Conversely, sharing bad dreams is common practice to ease the emotional burden by distributing the pain.

In various Native American cultures, including the Ojibwe, children on the verge of adolescence would go to a sacred, isolated place—such as a mountain or forest—where they would fast in small groups. This challenging trial involved confronting hunger, physical discomfort, and danger with the goal of receiving a dream visitation from a spirit helper and gaining wisdom. The spirit helper, often in animal form, would guide the child toward their role and responsibility within the larger community, teaching them how to share their strengths and gifts.

ABENAKI

According to the **Abenaki** people of northeastern North America, the world was created when the Great Spirit summoned a Turtle into being. The Great Spirit slathered the Turtle's shell with piles and piles of mud, which became the mountains and valleys of our Earth. Exhausted after all that work, the Great Spirit dozed off. While he slept, he dreamed all the creatures of the world into existence, populating this newly formed landscape of **Turtle Island**.

THE IMPACT OF COLONIZATION

Before European colonizers invaded the Americas, decimated communities, and forced the surviving Indigenous people to follow their laws and attend their schools, most tribal societies looked very different. The youth were educated holistically, working alongside elders, and experience was a primary method of learning. Many traditions were lost, devalued, criminalized, and destroyed under colonial rule, but these are still living cultures, and much of their wisdom has been preserved and passed on by survivors.

Learning more about how cultures of the past and present communicate with the dream realm can help expand and enrich your own understanding of it. Seeking out public Indigenous voices from around the world—authors, poets, artists, researchers, educators—supports keeping traditions alive and healthy and deepens individual practice. However, it's important to approach other cultures respectfully. The eclectic New Age dreamwork practices of the 1970s, in particular, tended to borrow from diverse cultures, especially Native American cultures, but without crediting them—cherry-picking interesting tidbits, making things up, and idealizing spiritual practices in ways that flattened their complexity. Many Indigenous activists have spoken out against the harm this approach has caused their sacred traditions.

SOUTH AMERICA

WORRY DOLLS

According to Mayan legend, the Sun God granted the Corn Goddess **Ixmucane** the power to solve any human problem. Today in Guatemala and Mexico, people make tiny dolls in the likeness of Ixmucane called **muñecas quitapenas**, or worry dolls, using wood or paper, wire, and scraps of fabric. The dolls are given to children, who tell their troubles to the dolls and place them under their pillows at night. While the children dream, their problems are solved by Princess Ixmucane.

ACHUAR COLLECTIVE DREAMING

The **Achuar** people of South America traditionally sleep communally in thatched huts, their rest punctuated by the sounds of animals and other disruptions. Because of this, waking life blends into dreaming, and dreaming weaves back into waking.

The ancestral practice of sharing dreams is integral to Achuar society. People gather several hours before dawn to discuss and interpret their dreams, sipping a caffeinated beverage called **guayusa** made from boiled leaves. Young children are included in these morning dream circles and taught how to use, interpret, and direct their dreams. A dream does not belong to the individual but to the community. If the meaning of a dream isn't determined during the morning dream circle, the individual carries the dream through the day's activities, hoping to figure it out.

In the 1990s, the Achuar people began dreaming about an impending danger to their communities as oil companies began encroaching on their territory, seeking to drill on their land. Largely influenced by their collective dreaming, the Achuar joined forces with other Indigenous peoples and international environmental justice organizations to protect their land from further exploitation. In more recent years, guayusa visions have continued to support the Achuar in seeking sustainable solutions, including using renewable energy to protect their land; however, as in much of Central and South America, foreign industry's extraction of resources is a constant threat to Indigenous land and peoples.

YANOMAMI

The Yanomami people of Brazil have a sacred relationship with dreaming, viewing sleeping and waking as interconnected realms. It is common, for example, for people to dream about which plants will provide cures to illnesses and for parents to dream the names of their babies, usually through an animal visitation. Dreaming is considered a way to connect outwardly, in contrast to the modern psychological approach that sees dreams as a tool to turn inward and learn about oneself. For the Yanomami, dreaming is a collective action—an exploratory adventure.

TUNAL

According to the Nawat people of Santo Domingo de Guzmán, El Salvador, one should avoid going to bed angry or stressed, as dreaming is a vulnerable time when the ***tunal,*** or spirit, leaves the body. During its nightly travels, the tunal can send the sleeper helpful messages and warnings using the language of symbols. If someone goes through a period of time without dreaming, it's a matter of concern, as this could indicate the tunal has gotten lost, which can lead to physical illness; in these cases, the tunal must be called back to the body through ritual.

CYCLE IX

BUILDING SKILLS

CYCLE IX WEEK 1  NEW MOON

ANIMAL CONNECTION

If you've ever watched a dog sleep, you may have noticed it moving as if chasing something in its dreams. Scientists who developed methods to monitor brain waves and eye movements in humans applied the same technologies to various animals. By attaching electrodes to the animals while they slept, researchers found that many animals' brains lit up in the same areas as those of dreaming humans. This led to the conclusion that mammals (and birds) also dream—and dream vividly.

Although our pets can't describe their dreams, brain scans suggest that animals likely process events from their waking lives, or practice skills to enhance their abilities. For instance, when puppies twitch, it's believed they are building their muscles during sleep.

CONSIDER:

Discovering that animals dream has significantly influenced our understanding of their intelligence. For a long time, it was thought that only certain animals, particularly primates and dolphins, were sentient—able to recognize their own existence. However, evidence suggests that most animals dream, raising profound questions about animal consciousness. If animals can dream, what other kinds of thoughts might they be capable of? Perhaps we humans are not as unique as we think.

EXPLORE:

Many animals hold symbolic meanings in different cultures. Lions, as apex predators, often embody a powerful, regal energy. Turtles, protected by their shells and moving slowly, evoke safety and deliberation. Birds, with their ability to fly, can represent liberation.

Review your dream journal and search for any animals that have appeared. Consider each animal from an archetypal perspective: What qualities does it possess?

* *How does it physically move through the world?*
* *What is your personal relationship with this animal?*
* *What do you think this animal brought to your dreaming life? Why do you think it appeared, and what can it bring to your waking life?*

Broadly speaking, animals represent primal instincts. Consider the health of the animal and its role in your dream. Could it represent you, or a quality in your life? Are there any animals that appear repeatedly in your dreams or waking life? Do you personally identify with any species?

Spend some time in a hypnagogic threshold state this week (see page 74) and meditate on an animal you're fond of—or allow your imagination to introduce one to you. In a relaxed state with your eyes closed, imagine the animal in its natural environment. Visualize it moving through its space. See if it has anything to show you.

Alternatively, experiment with embodying an animal by imagining you are looking through its eyes.

RATS

In a scientific study, researchers monitored rats' brains while they navigated a maze. Later, while the rats slept, the scientists observed their brain patterns again. They discovered that the same areas were activated in the rats' brains during sleep as when they were running through the maze, implying that the rats were dreaming about the maze. The observations were so precise that the scientists could pinpoint which part of the maze the dreaming rats were working through, based on which neurons were lighting up!

CUTTLEFISH

While we don't know what these underwater creatures think or dream about, something interesting must be going on in their slumbering minds, because they can change color while asleep.

It would appear that not only do men dream, but horses also, and dogs, and oxen; aye, and sheep, and goats, and all viviparous quadrupeds; and dogs show their dreaming by barking in their sleep.

—Aristotle

ZEBRA FINCHES

Birds aren't born knowing the songs they sing; they have to learn them. They practice these songs not only while they're awake but also while they're sleeping. Scientists have tracked which notes zebra finches sing in their dreams by noting the precise neurons that fire. They can even reconstruct and replay the birds' dream songs by mapping their sleeping brain waves.

PLAY:

Consider the power of dreams to connect one human consciousness to another—and what that means for animals who also dream.

If you have a pet, sit with your animal and try to connect with them mentally. Stare into their eyes and see if a bond develops. Take it further: Nap with your pet, resting your head near theirs. Set an intention to meet your animal in your dream, seeing if your relationship manifests in the dream realm. Maybe your animal has something to share with you in this alternate reality.

GO DEEPER

This week, pay particular attention to any animals you come across out in the world—squirrels, insects, birds, dogs. If you're interested in synchronicity, notice the context of your encounter: Where and when did you spot the animal? What qualities does it possess, and what associations do you have with the species? Perhaps the animal has something to communicate. If you can, spend a little time relating with them more consciously.

CYCLE IX WEEK 2 ◑ WAXING MOON

CONNECTING TO NATURE

Throughout this year, you may have explored some deep, untouched territory in your dreams. This can dredge up intense emotions that affect your waking life; the things we keep buried can cause disruption and discomfort when they're brought to surface. It's important to stay grounded and not become overwhelmed. One way to take care of yourself is by taking the idea of "grounding" literally: Remember your connection to this earthy planet, teeming with life.

PLAY:

This week, take some time to connect with nature beyond your usual routine. Find a patch of green, whether that involves going on a hike, eating lunch in a park, or working in a garden or greenhouse.

Observe some plants and draw or photograph them. Talk to a tree; reach out and touch its bark. Lie down in the grass. If it's winter and snowy where you are, bundle up and go for a walk, breathing in the crisp air.

Even if you live alone, you are constantly surrounded by living beings. Insects, plants, mammals, birds, rodents, even microorganisms that live on your skin and inside your body—all these life-forms coexist with you daily. And above you—while maybe not "alive" in the strict, scientific sense—the moon, sun, stars, and sky are also your companions.

This week, make an effort to communicate with these entities, expressing your appreciation for them.

CONSIDER:

Since ancient times, people have observed that some plants seem to go through sleeping and waking phases with the rising and setting of the sun. The official term for a plant's response to darkness is nyctinasty*, which you can see when a plant's flowers close or its leaves fold in tightly around its stalk. Some flowers even get their names from their tendencies to sleep or wake, such as morning glories and night jasmine.*

Just like us, plants use their senses to gather data from their environments and respond accordingly. However, since plants lack brains, the scientific consensus is that they cannot dream.

EXPLORE:

Plants that are consumed to induce or enhance dreaming are called **oneirogens**: "dream creators." From a modern perspective, these plants differ from drugs that alter our states of consciousness, because they affect the dreaming mind, not the waking sense of reality.

* ***Entada rheedii*** is a large climbing vine popular for its ability to induce vivid dreams. Found growing throughout tropical regions in Africa, Australia, and Asia, its pods can grow as tall as a person and contain seeds that are soaked in water or roasted before consumption. The seeds are so large that they can float on the ocean and drift to distant shores, which explains their widespread growth and use. In many places, they are used to make jewelry.
* ***Calea zacatechichi*** is a bitter plant used as a tea in Mexico and Central America to extend the REM stage of sleep and enhance dreaming.

You can grow, dry, and infuse many of the following herbs yourself—which will likely strengthen your connection to them—or find them in premade sleep-tea blends.

* **Mugwort** grows wild in disturbed earth and has folk uses for protection and dreaming. It can be eaten, smoked, brewed as tea, bent into wreaths (see page 51), or stuffed in dream pillows. However, be aware that mugwort is an **emmenagogue**, meaning it can encourage the menstrual cycle to start, so it should be avoided by pregnant people.
* **Chamomile** is a small flower with feathery green leaves, white petals, and a yellow center, known for its sweet apple-like scent and soothing, relaxing properties.
* **Valerian** is a flower whose pungent roots are used in tea for their sedative properties. It deepens sleep, enriches dreams, and helps with dream recall. Known colloquially as "nature's Valium," valerian root has long been used as an anxiety-relieving alternative to the addictive pharmaceutical drug.
* **Lavender** is a purple flower well-known for its strong floral scent and calming influence.

CONJURE:

Try to carry some of the lush green energy of the plant world into your dreams. Run your fingers through leaves before bed, commune with a houseplant, sketch your favorite flower, or imbibe an evening herbal infusion. Place an herbal sprig under your pillow or in your pajama pocket. Then, as you fall asleep, focus on your intention to dream of flora.

Remember: The language of dreams is subtle, often preferring hints, suggestions, and wordplay to direct answers. Sometimes you need to look closely to recognize responses to your requests. Try not to get frustrated by this enigmatic style of expression.

CYCLE IX WEEK 3 FULL MOON

ENVISIONING

In the English language, "to dream" is commonly used as a substitute for "to hope" and doesn't necessarily mean passively receiving sensory information in your sleep. We say, "In your dreams!" about something seemingly impossible, and we talk about "dreaming of a better tomorrow." Famously, Dr. Martin Luther King repeated the words "I have a dream . . ." in his 1963 Civil Rights speech imagining a more just and equitable United States.

Dreaming, in this sense, is an active and creative process that engages our waking, intellectual mind. It requires imagination. There is great power in envisioning the things you want to see in the world. Putting these aspirations into words—writing about them, talking about them with others—is even more potent. This is why art matters: Being able to imagine the future carries a degree of influence, and from there, you can work toward making it happen.

Dreams, in the sense we've mostly been discussing them—the experiences we have while asleep—can reinforce the goals we strive toward in our waking lives. They allow us to glimpse new realities as if they've already manifested. This can encourage us to make changes in our lives that help our visions come true.

CONSIDER:

*Aboriginal Australian researcher, community leader, and filmmaker **Dr. Anne Poelina** advocates for Earth and human rights from an Indigenous First Law perspective. As we explore more on page 124, Dreamtime is an Indigenous worldview that contains far more than just what happens when we sleep. In her paper (which lists the Martuwarra River as a coauthor) "Ancient Wisdom Dreaming a Climate Chance," Dr. Poelina writes:*

"We can Dream together so we can better understand how we, as human beings, can once again start to live in harmony with each other and with our non-human families. We need to enjoy and defend our amazing planet, Mother Earth, and life itself from climate chaos and destruction. Otherwise, Mother Earth will be lonely without the vibrations of human beings upon her girth! . . . Let us Dream and act now to transform our thinking and practice, and adapt to climate change, for a climate chance, for humanity in the future, and some sense of planetary well-being."

EXPLORE:

What would the future look like if you had more control over it? Consider this for you personally; for your family; for your community, city, and country; for the planet; for future generations; and for other-than-human life. Imagine what the world could be, and allow yourself to connect to something bigger than your own consciousness.

Focus on these aspirations before bed this week and see if you can find hope, support, or guidance in your sleep. Ask your dreams to offer purpose to your waking days, renewing and recharging your optimism. Dream to empower; dream to shift narratives; dream to sustain and nourish; dream to keep hope alive.

CHECK IN:

Have you noticed periods when your dreamwork has felt less inspired and more like a chore?

Like any great undertaking, dreamwork has its own natural rhythms, and your enthusiasm for it might ebb and flow. Try not to get too distressed when you lose motivation, but don't let your work come to a halt, either. Pay attention to factors that might contribute to your loss of momentum—busyness? Boredom? The season? But don't overthink it.

If you're lacking the energy to record your dreams, try making single-word entries for a while. Pick things back up when you're ready, or reinvigorate your work with a ritual at the next full moon.

PRAYER

People around the world use words as spiritual aids in the form of prayers and mantras to communicate with higher powers, ask for help, and find peace. When hope feels hard to hold on to, prayer is a simple action that can sustain you.

Find or create a word, phrase, or short prayer that you can turn to before sleep to ground yourself. Think of these words as an amulet that can soothe and protect you. Carry your prayer with you into sleep and find it again in your dreams. Return to these words upon waking.

This can also be a useful tactic if you're having trouble falling asleep, or if you wake up in the middle of the night feeling unsettled.

The *Compline*, also known as the Night Prayer, is the last liturgy of the day in Catholic tradition, formally closing out the day with a request for spiritual peace and protection throughout the night. After it is completed, silence and contemplation are invited in.

CYCLE IX WEEK 4 ◐ WANING MOON

TRANSLATION AND DECODING

We've all had dreams during which we wake up wondering: *What did that mean? What is the universe trying to tell me?* Dreams are a way the cosmos communicates with us, but sometimes it can feel like something's gotten lost in translation.

Referring to the map you created in Cycle II, Week 2 can help jog associations about who or what a dream might be referring to. It can also be helpful to interview yourself and the dream, asking some basic questions for clarity.

MESSAGES AND THEMES

* Did anyone speak to you in your dream? Was there any writing or explicit communication? Sometimes, the theme is unspoken but obvious—being chased, for example, or going on a journey—while other times it's subtler and harder to tease out.

  Try summing up your dream in one sentence, then read it back to yourself. Does anything "click" for you? Entertain the idea that the sentence may be personally meaningful, even if you don't understand its meaning yet. Write it down and carry it with you. See if a deeper resonance reveals itself.

SETTING

* Where did the dream take place? What are your associations with this kind of environment? How spacious was the landscape—did it feel similar to something you might encounter in your waking life?

EMOTIONAL TONE

* Often, one of the more lingering qualities of a dream is how it makes you feel. A dream can leave strong emotional residues, so note how you feel when you first wake up: Well rested? Scared, anxious, or amused? How does your *body* feel—tense, relaxed, sore? Your physical response might hold some clues to your emotional experience, so take time to check in with yourself.

CHARACTERS

* What beings—humans, animals, animated objects—populated your dream? What was your relationship to them, and how did your interactions go? What might they represent?

OBJECTS AND IMAGES

* Work with your personal symbol dictionary (page 66) to discern possible meanings for different objects or images in your dream. Using the self-interview method, ask questions like: *What does this object or image remind me of? Does it have cultural or religious significance? Where did I find it, and how is it used?*

PLAY:

For fun, explore the seemingly arbitrary nature of dream symbols, imagining that every person or object in your dream represents something else, almost like a secret code. That mouse? It's your father! That bowl of spaghetti? It's the chaos in your life. Dream symbolism can be absurd at times—but even that absurdity can yield insight.

Return to a recent dream entry, circle all the nouns, and copy them onto a blank page. Now rewrite the dream by swapping the nouns. If your original entry reads: "Biking to the beach, a coyote trots by as I go under the bridge," you could change it to: "Biking to the coyote! A bridge trots by as the beach rolls under me." Feel free to adjust the punctuation and some of the other words in each sentence to make better or more interesting sense. You decide whether you're seeking deeper understanding, a more poetic creation, or some combination of both.

REFLECT:

According to Jungian dream theory, every character and object in your dreams represents an aspect of yourself, and you embody each of them. To experiment with this concept, revisit a memorable dream in your journal and imagine yourself as another character or object you encountered. For instance, if you dreamed about turning on a lamp, consider that you are also the lamp. Reflect on what it means for you to be "lit up" or "turned on."

Remember: Dreams love wordplay and puns!

EXPLORE:

While it's often satisfying to decode recent dreams, try digging deeper into your archives, uncovering a dream in your journal that you may not even remember having. These forgotten dreams are especially ripe for analysis, as you can approach them with fresh eyes and greater objectivity.

DREAMING JOURNEY:
AUSTRALIA

Tjukurrpa in the Warlpiri language; *Bookarrarra* in the Nyikina Warrwa language; *Nura* in the Dharug language. These are names the Indigenous peoples of Australia give to their primary worldview, which translates as "Dreamtime" or "Ancestral Order" in English.

Dreamtime differs dramatically from the linear Western imperial worldview. It contains all the stories, knowledge, ceremonies, and customs practiced across Australia. While some beliefs vary by tribe and community, commonalities exist. In the Dreamtime creation story, the ancestors descended from the sky and emerged from the earth to sing the world into existence. They eventually settled into landforms—mountains, rivers, cliffs, and the earth itself—and their spirits still reside alongside, beneath, and above us.

In the Dreamtime worldview, creation isn't a discrete past event; it is perpetually unfolding. The universe is believed to be fully alive and eternal, and time is circular, with past, present, and future existing simultaneously. Similarly, personhood extends beyond humans to include animals, plants, the land, rocks, rivers, planets, and stars—everything.

DEFINING TERMS

To the Warlpiri people of the Tanami Desert, ***Tjukurrpa*** (collective dreaming) is distinct from ***kapukurri*** (nightly dreaming), but the two are connected. Nightly dreams are the visions people experience while they sleep, which link them to the much vaster Dreamtime, the cultural worldview that encompasses all Aboriginal beliefs, art, rules, and culture. The terms are not interchangeable: While nightly dreams are a powerful component of Dreamtime, they are just one strand of it.

Dreams are more than symbolic narratives to interpret; they are tools that connect humans, animals, land, and all other beings to one another. In the Yolngu Dreamtime, for instance, dreams provide guidance on how to relate to the rest of the natural world, teaching sustainability and conservation of our planet's resources and cohabitors. Dreams can also deliver songs, art, and rituals to people while they sleep.

Everyone plays a part in creation through dreaming. Children emerge from Dreamtime into this earthly realm when their mother or another close family member first dreams about them—and when a person dies, they journey back into *Tjukurrpa*.

CYCLE X

DREAM PLAY

CYCLE X WEEK 1 ◯ NEW MOON

DISRUPTING SLEEP

Early on in this atlas, we emphasized the benefits of creating a regular sleep routine. Once in a while, however, a change in routine can freshen your experience, especially when the change is intentional. After all, dreamwork can disrupt the rigid patterns of daily habits and reinvigorate your imagination. This week, we will turn dreams' tricks on themselves and shake up your established sleep routine.

According to European folklore, the **witching hour** occurs in the wee hours of the morning, around 3 a.m., when the supernatural awakens and witchcraft is at its most potent. When a person wakes up during this time, they are often agitated and uneasy, their waking-life stresses somehow seeming more dire. Otherworldly explanations aside, this is likely due to the physiological effects of disrupted REM sleep, which can cause bodily dysregulation.

PREINDUSTRIAL WAKEFULNESS

What we now consider sleep "disruptions" weren't always so. In the days before electricity, humans' sleep schedules were more closely aligned with natural darkness—but they didn't sleep straight through the night. For many generations, there were two phases of sleep. People would settle into bed as the sun set and sleep until around midnight. At that time, they'd wake up, and in a somnolent state, snack, make love, pray, think, read, or do simple chores. Then they'd fall back asleep for a second rest until morning. This **segmented sleep** (or **polyphasic sleep**) was typical up until the invention of electricity, when technology dramatically impacted our experience of nightfall and darkness.

More recent studies have explored segmented sleep in a modern context, and most researchers agree that the amount of sleep is what's crucial: As long as you're sleeping for eight hours or so, it doesn't matter if you break them up or get them in one solid chunk. In fact, segmented sleep has been known to help people with chronic insomnia, alleviating some of the pressure associated with lying awake at night by allowing more options.

EXPLORE:

Experiment with disruption without leaving your home:

* **Shift your orientation.** Sleep on the opposite end of the bed, placing your head where your feet usually go—or move your bed, setting it against a different wall.
* **Change your room or sleep surface.** Sleep on a couch in the living room, or stay in your bedroom but move to the floor and tuck into a sleeping bag.

* **Mix up your schedule.** You'll want to reserve these experiments for nights when you don't have many responsibilities the next day, as they may affect your physical and mental alertness.

    * Set your alarm for ninety minutes earlier than you normally wake up; this will prevent you from entering your final REM phase of sleep. Later, make time for a nap in the middle of the day. Napping dreams can be especially vivid, so this is sometimes a shortcut to a more intense dreaming experience.
    * Alternatively, set your alarm to wake you in the middle of the night, around 3 a.m.—the witching hour. Spend some time with the darkness around you, noticing its distinctive qualities. If you feel heightened anxiety, remind yourself that this is part of the territory; it will likely lighten up when you next wake.

PLAY:

The ancient Greeks embarked on pilgrimages to mountaintop temples to incubate dreams. Others throughout time have visited caves, graveyards, and other sacred places to imbue their sleep with mystical energy—see page 137 for more examples.

Are there any places you feel called to dream inside?

When you sleep somewhere new, do so with the awareness that your environment can influence your dreams. If you can, plan a dream retreat: Sleep outside under the stars or spend the night in an unfamiliar location. This doesn't have to be a costly getaway—ask a friend or relative if you can stay over at their place, or set up a hammock in a nearby park for an afternoon nap.

Leonardo da Vinci developed a polyphasic sleep practice that some believe contributed to his remarkable productivity. Instead of sleeping a total of eight hours at night, he is said to have taken twenty-minute naps every four hours—adding up to just two hours of sleep per day. Inspired by da Vinci, **Thomas Edison** followed a similar sleep schedule, taking six half-hour naps each day for a total of three hours of sleep. Although Edison dismissed sleep as superfluous, his own invention of the commercial light bulb would, ironically, go on to transform our relationship to darkness, making longer stretches of sleep more common.

Lest you think the secret to genius lies in unconventional sleep patterns, think again: **Albert Einstein** treasured his sleep and made sure he clocked ten hours a night, even adding the occasional daytime nap. Besides, some theorize that a genetic mutation may have contributed to da Vinci's decreased need for sleep—a rare condition that makes sleep more efficient for certain individuals, allowing them to feel well rested on much less sleep than most of us need.

CYCLE X WEEK 2 ◑ WAXING MOON

LUCID DREAMING

Lucid dreaming is the ability to consciously control what happens in your dreams; some people describe it as being "awake" while sleeping. The Christian theologian **Saint Augustine of Hippo** described lucid dreaming as a preview of the afterlife.

The first step to achieving lucidity in dreams is to realize that you are, in fact, dreaming. For some, this is enough. Others may be inclined to go further and experiment with actively controlling and directing their dreams.

EXPLORE:

You've probably heard or used the expression "Somebody pinch me!" when something seems too good to be true—too much like a dream. Pinching oneself in this case is a method of **reality checking**: If you feel the pinch, you must *not* be dreaming. However, this is not the most effective form of reality checking, as we can experience physical sensations in our dreams (see Cycle III, Week 3).

To become more adept at realizing you're dreaming, practice reality checks throughout the day. Regularly ask yourself: *Am I dreaming?* You might want to set reminders or make a plan to check in with yourself every hour, on the hour. Look at your hands and count your fingers. Are they all there? No extras? Do they look normal? Practice this often enough in your waking life, and you might begin to carry the habit into your dreams.

Other options for reality checks:

* **Pinch your nose shut and close your mouth.** Can you still breathe?
* **Check your pulse.** Can you feel a steady beat?
* **Look at your face in a mirror.** Is that you? Does everything look normal?

One of the first steps to lucidity is noticing that something is off. While developing these skills, you might suddenly realize you're doing something impossible in your dreams—that you're interacting with someone who's supposed to be dead, for example. You may rationalize the confusion away and continue the dream as normal, but sometimes the realization can be so jarring that you wake up. This is a victory! Keep it up, and maybe next time, instead of waking up, you can continue the dream, holding on to your awareness and maybe even introducing more control over what you experience.

As with dream incubation, it can be helpful to write down your lucidity goals before falling asleep. Start small, and as you progress, move toward larger and larger goals, eventually aiming for full, conscious control.

* **GOAL 1:** I will realize I am dreaming.

* **GOAL 2:** I will realize I am dreaming and will remain inside the dream with this newfound awareness.

* **GOAL 3:** I will realize I am dreaming and be able to consciously take control of my dream.

PLAY:

Once you've achieved some degree of lucidity, you may want to combine dream incubation with lucid dreaming practices by attempting to visit various locations. Before bed, set a goal for your dream-self to arrive at a specific place, such as a library, forest, or village. If you succeed, try to revisit this place repeatedly, using your senses to explore it further and in more detail.

The results of increasing awareness in the dreamworld can carry over into your waking life, bringing more mindfulness to your day-to-day. However, be aware that lucid dreaming can interfere with truly restful sleep, so it's best to attempt it in moderation.

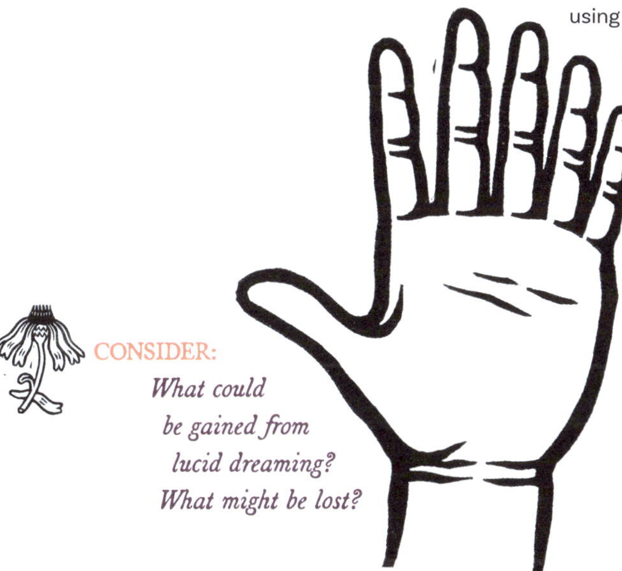

CONSIDER:

What could be gained from lucid dreaming? What might be lost?

CONTROL AND SURRENDER

We naturally desire agency over our lives: the ability and freedom to make meaningful choices about how we spend our time. Of course, sometimes our freedoms may feel limited for a number of reasons—some societal or institutional in nature, others financial or familial, mental or physical.

For many, dreaming offers the promise of limitless possibility: a space of radical creation, of conjuring something out of nothing. In this sense, we can access tremendous, almost godlike power in our dreams. However, sleep is also a passive, restorative time. Last week, we leaned into the creative power of lucid dreaming, but this week, we'll explore the benefits of surrender and acceptance.

To surrender is to be at the mercy of forces beyond yourself—to accept being an object as much as a subject. We may not know exactly why we dream, but we have evolved to experience these nightly reveries during which we relinquish decision-making and are humbled to simply exist. Perhaps this is a quality of dreaming we can respect and appreciate, rather than resist or deny. As profound as lucidity can be, we might find equal nourishment in its opposite—in allowing our dreams to flow through us as needed.

CONSIDER:

Some cultures and dispositions emphasize success and goal-setting, while others encourage acceptance and living in the present moment. Meanwhile, many of us are simply making ends meet—striving to keep safe, or even just to survive. In your own culture, is goal-setting (a form of control) valued over presence (a form of surrender)? Are they equally celebrated? How about you, personally—where do you tend to fall on this spectrum, or how do you move around in it?

EXPLORE:

This week, in your waking life, notice opportunities to not react, instead letting a situation unfold without your involvement or direction. This can be a potent exercise during moments of interpersonal conflict, when our instincts and emotions tend to guide us. Consciously slowing down in these moments allows time for things to play out and perhaps cool off, giving you a chance to respond more thoughtfully and rationally—or, if appropriate, not at all.

PLAY:

How does surrender feel in your body? If you can, experiment with positions of physical surrender and release this week. Before bed, spend several minutes in **child's pose**: kneeling, resting your seat between your heels, then folding forward onto your thighs with your arms in front of you, your forehead touching the ground or a pillow. Alternatively, lie flat on your back in **corpse pose**: your arms at your sides, your palms facing up. Allow your muscles to slacken, sinking your full weight into the ground. Notice sensations of release, of passivity, and appreciate their effect on your body. Let the earth hold you.

CHECK IN:

This week, consciously surrender your dreams to the ether. Don't write them down; instead, allow them to evaporate like the morning dew. Your dreams will continue to benefit you, even if you don't remember them.

Surrender—physical or emotional—isn't always comfortable or easy. For some, it might activate feelings of deep unease, vulnerability, or shame. In a safe, supportive space, allow your body to accept or endure these feelings of discomfort. With practice, surrender may begin to feel more tolerable, perhaps even translating to a spiritual release.

When you value both control and surrender, you can come to a deeper awareness of which energy best serves you in a given situation.

CYCLE X WEEK 4 ◐ WANING MOON

DREAMS AND TECHNOLOGY

The internet has a lot in common with the dreamworld: loose boundaries, remote interpersonal interactions, lack of physicality, and the ability to provide information instantaneously, to name a few similarities. Perhaps unsurprisingly, companies and apps have sought to capitalize on this realm, creating trackers, databases, and platforms for influencers and consumers interested in dreamwork. Yet our dreamworld is one of the few places in modern life where we are free from advertisements and the hustle of the attention economy—unless, of course, we dream about these things.

CATALOGING THEMES

The subject matter of our dreams has been collected and studied at least since ancient Greece, when Artemidorus recorded people's dreams by hand. Starting in the 1940s, scholars **Calvin S. Hall** and **Robert Van de Castle** took up that lofty mission, compiling common dream data from around the world, gathering over 50,000 reports across three decades. They developed a quantitative coding system that analyzes dreams for content, not meaning. In the Hall/Van de Castle system, common dream elements are assigned individual codes, and that data can be used to compare dreams across populations.

Researchers are often interested in gathering dream data during specific points in history, such as during or after war or major disaster, to investigate how our collective unconscious processes these events.

*In 2019, Martha Crawford launched the **Climate Dreams Project**, an online platform where people can submit dreams they've had about climate change. This collection reveals ways the planet in crisis is making its way into collective consciousness. It also reveals that younger generations, people of color, and inhabitants of high-impact areas like the western United States are significantly more likely to report climate change-related dreams.*

DREAMING APPS AND ARTIFICIAL INTELLIGENCE

Recently, mobile apps that provide music and soundscapes, gentle alarms, sleep-tracking technology, and features for users to record and share their dreams have hit the market. Some apps draw keywords from digital dream journal entries, using AI predictive models to generate imagery based on them. Others are specifically designed to help people have lucid dreams, providing step-by-step lessons and objectives.

While the ability to instantly visualize and share any fleeting thought may sound like a dream come true, it's important to note that AI requires a tremendous amount of electricity and water to operate, putting a profound strain on our planet's resources.

When we submit our intimate, detailed dreams to these apps, we receive a generalized corporate average in return. Moreover, these models are often trained using the original art and writing of human creators—usually without permission.

CONTEMPORARY DREAM STUDIES

In recent years, sleep scientists have leveraged new technological advancements to analyze the inner workings and potential uses of dreams.

In 2020, researchers at the MIT Media Lab published a study on what they called **targeted dream incubation (TDI)**. Test subjects wore devices that tracked their sleep cycles, and while the subjects were in the suggestible hypnagogic state, the devices played recordings of provocative phrases that influenced many of the subjects' dreams.

In an earlier study at the University of California, Berkeley, researchers showed video clips to test subjects while measuring and tracking their brain activity. A computer then used this data to re-create an accurate, albeit abstract, visual representation of what the subjects had seen. Researchers project that this technology could someday be used to reproduce an individual's dreams.

CONSIDER:

What do we stand to gain or lose by outsourcing our dreamwork to a machine? How about one that's been trained using unethical practices and is unsustainably powered by our planet's natural resources?

PLAY:

What are your thoughts about future dream technologies? Would you be interested in having your brain monitored by scientists who can manipulate or re-create your dreams? Would you want to enter someone else's dreams, or have lucidity bolstered by science? What happens when artificial intelligence meets the spiritual world of dreams?

Imagine a hypothetical way dreams and technology could be combined. If you're inspired, develop your daydream into a piece of **flash fiction** (under five hundred words) or a short story. These frontiers can be fertile ground for artistic generation—or for exploring dystopian anxieties.

> **Yumemi Kobo** is a Japanese invention designed to allow dreamers to control their dreams—a lucid dreaming technology aid. The dreamer uploads photos of what they wish to dream about, selects a fragrance and music, and records a verbal description of their desired dream. Once the sleeper is in the REM state, the machine emits a blinking light, releases the chosen scent and background music, and repeats the keywords the dreamer fed to it earlier. After eight hours, the gadget gently wakes the sleeper so the experience can be remembered.

EXPLORE:

This week, check out an online dream repository such as the **Sleep and Dream Database**, started by dream expert Dr. Kelly Bulkeley, or the **DreamBank**, run by Adam Schneider and G. William Domhoff. These resources are used for scientific inquiry, but anyone can access and play with them.

CONJURE:

In times of rapid change and upheaval, anxieties mount. Yet dreams endure, essential to our humanity. Cherish them. Ask them to kindle a sense of calm and purpose in you. Consider asking your dreams for wisdom, clarity, or confidence to guide you through periods of uncertainty.

DREAMING JOURNEY:
EUROPE

A CROSS-CULTURAL STORY

The tale of **Seven Sleepers** (also called the Companions of the Cave) dates back as far as ancient Greece, and appears in the Qur'an and in medieval retellings. Versions of it have been told in Irish, Ethiopic, Armenian, Georgian, and more. While details and descriptions vary from story to story, there are always a number of brothers—sometimes with a dog in tow—who flee persecution and end up in a cave. There, they fall asleep for approximately three hundred years. When they awaken, the entire world has changed.

Why is this tale of prolonged, time-defying sleep so fascinating to people? In some ways, it reminds us how quickly things can change in our society. Think of how different the world was even five years ago, much less twenty, or three hundred. Maybe, the idea of waking up many years in the future appeals as an alternative to keeping up with the rapid pace of our modern world; it's an opportunity to let go, allowing the current of time to bear us downstream.

NORSE CULTURE

The Norse people of Scandinavia believed in preordained destiny: that the future was fixed and certain, and therefore knowable. Dreams were a way to access that information and were believed to possess the power of prophecy—which meant they were taken seriously. Often, if someone needed to receive important, elusive information, the message would come to them in a dream, in the form of poetry. These poems came from the gods, which explained why people with modest artistic skill could still share profound messages. Sleeping on grave mounds or wrapping oneself in animal hides were ways to induce this poetic revelation, connecting the dreamer to the spirit world.

RUSSIAN AND SLAVIC CULTURES

In Russia and many Eastern European cultures, pagan beliefs understood dreams as channels to the ancestral and spiritual realms. Different deities brought different types of dreams according to their domains: **Mokosh**, the goddess of fertility, would bring nourishing dreams; **Morozko**, the winter god, would bring dreams of cold; and **Vodyanoy**, god of water, would bring vengeful dreams on those who disrespected nature. These dreams often shared warnings and guidance, so it was important to heed them. Dreaming was a lifebridge between the seen and unseen realms, and people would make offerings of food, flowers, and crafts to encourage meaningful dreams. For generations, stories and folk wisdom were shared orally, but in the 1800s, people began writing down and compiling the tales. This time period also saw the printing of ***sonniki***, dream dictionaries that documented the region's unique Slavic symbology.

In Slavic sonniki, dreaming of a large cat presages sorrow or disaster—especially the breaking of marriage vows: a cat is a bird thief, and birds resemble women, so dreaming about a cat symbolizes adultery. In general, the Slavic dream books don't offer reasoning behind their symbolism, but this is an exception, as it has likely traveled through history, originating in Artemidorus's Oneirocritica.

CELTIC CULTURE

Traditionally, the **Otherworld**, or spirit world, is said to exist alongside (but mostly hidden from) the earthly realm. At certain times of the year—particularly around October 31, the Celtic New Year known as **Samhain**—the veil that separates our realms grows thin, and the spirits of the Otherworld are more visible on this side. During this time, dreams might seem unusually intense or vivid, or they may include visitations from spirits and ancestors.

In Irish legend, divine dreams were sometimes solicited, especially by warrior-heroes. In the company of kings and druids, the seeker would prepare for the dream through meditation, purification, and sacrifice; it was considered dangerous to ask for divine revelations without performing the proper rites. Certain places—like riverbanks or the crests of earthen mounds—were considered ideal for sacred dream incubation.

The Irish word for "dream" is **aisling**, which is also the name of a genre of Irish poetry known as the "vision poem": a blend of that love poem, prophetic poem, and political poem. In aisling poetry, an Otherworldly female spirit (often an embodiment of Ireland herself) makes an appearance, bringing words of wisdom, songs of sorrow, and insight into the past and future.

In Celtic folk tradition, there are many dream spells and charms for introducing the sleeper to their true love. One such practice is to eat salted fish before bed—if you do, your true love will visit your dreams and offer you water to quench your thirst.

MODERNIZATION

During Europe's **Age of Enlightenment**, from the seventeenth to nineteenth centuries, logic and rationality were held in high regard, while the ambiguous, enigmatic world of dreams was generally ignored or deemed nonsense. However, since dreams are such an integral part of human experience, their influence was never completely eradicated. Many folk customs throughout Europe remained woven into the fabric of daily life—albeit often recast as superstition and taken with a grain of salt.

Though their cultural significance may ebb and flow, dreams are always with us.

CYCLE XI

DREAM MAGIC

PLAYING WITH TIME

Imagine watching a loved one sleep—observing the rise and fall of a few deep breaths, the slight flicker of eyes beneath closed lids. From your perspective, only a moment passes, yet in the mind of the sleeper, entire eras may elapse. Time in dreams is not always linear; it doesn't merely move forward. One can dream of simultaneous realities, intricately layered and folded upon each other; time can spiral back in on itself, with past, present, and future intertwining, each taking turns or speaking all at once.

Our perception of time is largely cultural. Ticking clocks and calendar pages may seem solid and universal, but these structures are relatively recent inventions and not the only ways of marking time today.

__Standardized time__ was invented as recently as 1883, during the Industrial Revolution, to keep trains on schedule; before that, towns and cities each had their own time.

While much of the modern world employs the Gregorian calendar, we've been using a lunar calendar throughout this book. Some cultures, like Igbo, Yoruba, and Javan, organize weeks based on worship and market days. We take it for granted that there's a certain way to organize or think about time, but dreams remind us that these systems are largely societal constructs, even if inspired by nature.

INDIVIDUAL PERCEPTION

On a more personal level, each of us experiences time a little differently, depending on a number of factors, including our emotional and psychological state, our attention and focus, and even our age. You may remember how, as a child, summer days could drag on almost eternally when you had nothing to do—whereas time spent immersed in a favorite activity could seem to pass all too quickly. There's even a word for the perception of time: **chronoception**.

Researchers theorize that the size of an animal and the rate of its metabolism influence how it experiences time: For a smaller animal with a naturally faster metabolic rate, time moves more slowly. Often, this also means they are quicker and more agile—if they perceive the world moving more slowly, they can respond to it more immediately.

It's not uncommon for humans to experience time-related illusions. In a phenomenon known as the **telescoping effect**, we tend to think that relatively recent events happened much longer ago, and vice versa. Drugs can also alter our perception of time, as can intense emotion: When we feel great awe or fear, time seems to slow down and expand around us.

As we age, our experience of time accelerates. At ten years old, a year represents one-tenth of our life, but as we accumulate years, each one feels a little shorter.

REFLECT:

Seconds, minutes, hours. Years, decades, centuries. Time in dreams is not so neat.

Which of these phenomena have occurred in your dreams?

* Simultaneous awareness of multiple happenings
* An ending
* A beginning
* **Circularity** (a recursive experience of time)
* **Premonition** (awareness of future events)
* **Anemoia** (awareness of past events you did not physically experience)
* The appearance of a clock or calendar

EXPLORE:

You'll need a friend for this activity. Take a comfortable seat and remain still, cuing your friend to start a stopwatch. When you think two minutes have passed, say "Stop!" Your friend will tell you how close you are to the actual two-minute mark.

Now try again, only this time, aim to mark five minutes.

Finally, have your friend start the stopwatch, but instead of sitting quietly, try reading an engaging book. Once you believe that five minutes have elapsed, say "Stop!" again.

What did you notice about the quality and duration of each experiment? Feel free to tinker with the activity to deepen your understanding of your own chronoception.

PLAY:

Argentinian author **Julio Cortázar** wrote that when someone gifts you with a watch, they are really presenting you with an obligation—"a tiny, flowering hell."

Untether yourself from time! Leave your phone and watch at home and remain unencumbered by the ticking clock for as long as you can. How does this change the quality of your experience?

Perhaps experimenting with time this week—in dreams and in waking life—will help expand the ways you use, fill, and experience it.

CONSIDER:

Pay attention to the quality of time in your dreams—how it passes, as well as "where" in time you are. Consider the ways past, present, and future can fold and overlap in dreams. Imagine what such an overlap would feel or look like in waking life.

CONJURE:

Use your dreams to time-travel. Set a dream intention to visit a specific time in history or in the future. If you want to visit the past, look at pictures or artifacts from that time period before bed. If you want to peek at the future, write a future date in your dream journal, or look at a calendar of the year you're curious about.

CYCLE XI WEEK 2 ◑ WAXING MOON

PROBLEM-SOLVING

As you continue to develop your dreamwork practice, you may find yourself struggling with a problem in your waking life. When this happens, return to the dream incubation techniques we explored in Cycle VI and see if you can program your dreams to help you work through the issue. This is where the balance between surrender and control becomes most important. You may pose a question in your dreamworld, but you can't dictate the outcome or answer you receive. Don't try to force it: Enter, your dream with trust and allow the revelation to come to you.

THE COMPLEXITIES OF HEALING

In ancient Greece, those who undertook the arduous pilgrimage to the temple of Asclepius, the god of healing, experienced healing in various forms. Sometimes, their dreams revealed how to treat their illness or resolve their problem. Other times, the ritual itself—climbing the mountain to the temple, bathing, being anointed by the priests, and sleeping in the sacred place—was enough to heal them.

While "healing" can be a loaded term, dreams at the very least offer potential for insight, support, and comfort. It would be nice if dreams could reliably solve all our problems, but in reality, immediate fixes are rare. The surest way forward involves addressing the situation and working slowly over time with a variety of methods—adapting to what is acceptable and striving to change what is not. Dreams can be one valuable tool along this journey.

CONSIDER:

Don't be discouraged if your dreams take an emotional turn when you're working on a problem:

That means you're making progress. You may wake up raw and sensitive from your night's work, but it means you're facing things and getting closer to resolution. When people with chronic depression are trapped in a depressive state, they generally report pleasant dreams. It's only once they start working to emerge from depression that their dreams become challenging and uncomfortable.

PLAY:

To practice using your dreams to solve problems, try asking them for help with riddles. The subconscious can provide answers your conscious mind might overlook or get stuck on. When the brain is in a hypnagogic state, it's more fluid, relaxed, and open to associations, which lends itself to innovative solutions. Intuition takes the driver's seat; logic and discernment move to the back.

Read one of these riddles one night just before bed. Don't try to solve it while you're awake; you don't want to apply your thinking mind. Instead, see if an answer comes to you in your dreams.

If you don't receive the answer, try not to get discouraged. Move on to another riddle or a different exercise. After all, frustration and stubbornness can hinder the natural flexibility of the dreamworld.

1st WHEN I FACE YOU FULL ON
I appear to bare everything,
but it's only half the story.
I slowly turn away,
leaving you with a smile
that fades into darkness.

2d I'M NOT HOT,
BUT I CAN BURN—
I am a crystal that forms
or slips away
at the mercy of gold.

3d I GROW
the less you feed me.

EXPLORE:

Now nearing a year of dreamwork, you've sufficiently strengthened your relationship to your dreams. It may even resemble a friendship. When you're facing a dilemma, can you turn to your dreams as you would a trusted friend?

Before sleep, try to ease into a relaxed headspace, taking some mindful breaths and perhaps sipping a cup of soothing sleep tea.

* Write down, or speak, your request for guidance: *Dreams, please help me with [dilemma] tonight.*
* Avoid focusing on the negative emotions associated with your problem, as they may weigh you down with frustration, which can lead to an anxiety or stress dream. Instead, let it all go, resting assured that your dreams will come through for you. Have faith in them.
* Upon waking, record your dream, even if it doesn't appear to respond to your problem. In time, and perhaps upon further reflection, you may discover hints that help you understand your situation differently, opening you up to a solution. Sometimes, you might simply awaken with a sense of clarity.

Some athletes use dreams to improve performance. Golf legend **Jack Nicklaus** sought the perfect swing, obsessing over it to the point that he would give himself lessons in his sleep. In one such dream, he was holding his club more loosely, and when he swung, the ball went soaring. He took this dream guidance to the green, relaxing his grip, and his game noticeably improved.

CYCLE XI WEEK 3 FULL MOON

DREAM SPELLS

Salvador Dalí, the renowned Spanish Surrealist, harnessed the power of dreams to shape his life and art. Drawing on his unique sense of humor and interest in the occult, he devised spells to tap into his dreams and overcome artist's block. In his illustrated book *50 Secrets of Magic Craftsmanship*, he shared several dream spells designed to conjure inspiration.

While most Surrealists used dreams and art to inspire liberatory visions for society, Dalí proclaimed himself apolitical and had a fascination with fascism that others in the movement found unacceptable. In 1934, his peer André Breton put Dalí on "trial," accusing him of glorifying Hitler; Dalí was expelled from the movement as a result.

PLAY:

Dalí's dream spell "Slumber with a Key" declares that sleeping for less than one minute will yield the most vivid, useful dreams. Dalí instructs us to fall asleep in a chair with a key in hand and a plate on the floor—as we drift into sleep, we'll drop the key, and when it falls into the dish, the resulting clatter will wake us.

Another of Dalí's spells for creative inspiration calls for eating three dozen sea urchins, collaborating with the moon in May, then dozing off in a soft armchair.

EXPLORE:

This week, experiment with different types of spells: writing them down, trying them out, seeing what kind of effect they have on your dreams or artistic practice. To cast your spell, you can get as bizarre, fanciful, poetic, or practical as you like.

Channel your inner Surrealist. Think of this dream-spell experiment as a combination of dream incubation and problem-solving, with a heaping measure of the strange baked into the recipe.

* **Identify your aim.** Decide what your spell will accomplish.
* **Collect three or four objects at random** (or intentionally, if you must). These objects might come from inside your home or from nature. They need not have any special meaning or any relationship to one another.

HINT: *Recall the assemblage-making exercise on page 94; this is a more performative version of that.*

* **Improvise a ritual involving all the objects.** Let's say you gathered an onion, a spoon, a flower, and a shoe. Now what? Perhaps you peel the onion with the spoon, throw it in the shoe, add the flower, petal by petal, don the shoe, and that a one-footed jig. Or maybe you eat the flower while balancing the spoon on your nose, rub the onion up and down your arms, and put the shoe on your head.

OR . . . ?

If a Surrealist approach doesn't call to you tonight, try out this more traditional spell format:

* **Decide on your intention.** What do you hope to call forth, achieve, or figure out? Condense this goal into a single word or short phrase.
* **Gather your supplies.** Bring the following items to your dream altar or another clear surface: a candle, a toothpick or permanent marker, your dream oil (see page 34), and a match or lighter.
* **Inscribe the candle with your intention.** You can carve your intention into the wax with a toothpick or, if the candle is encased in glass or a tin, you can write your goal on the container wit a permanent marker.
* **Dress the candle,** rubbing a bit of your dream oil into the wax.
* **Speak your intention aloud.** With your candle unlit, announce your intention, perhaps addressing a dream spirit, asking for guidance or a message.
* **Light the candle.** Spend a few moments with the flame, meditating on your intention.

CONSIDER:

The Surrealists believed in the shared ability of dreams and art to liberate the mind and being. For Dalí, sometimes that was best achieved through silliness.

Silliness isn't for everyone, and luckily, it isn't the only way to lighten up. Even if you're feeling constrained or burdened in your life, you can take small steps to give yourself more breathing room. Name what you are seeking and visualize it. Call it to your dreams and welcome it into your life. Dreams offer visions of expansive freedom—for ourselves, and for all.

CYCLE XI WEEK 4 WANING MOON

WORKING WITH CYCLES

Throughout this book, we've been working with attention to the monthly cycles of the moon, but there are other natural cycles we can align with, too—Earth's orbit around the sun, for instance, and the seasons it passes through as it orbits; the dance the stars and planets choreograph across the night sky. Notice and appreciate changes in the world around you, and observe how aligning with the patterns of the cosmos influences your dreaming.

Dreaming and Earth's rhythms are two guides, inviting us toward our purpose as a part of something bigger.

THE WHEEL OF THE YEAR

It takes Earth approximately 365 days to journey around the sun. During this time, the planet cycles through rhythms of light and dark, warmth and coolness—in other words, seasons. When our portion of the planet is angled toward the sun, the days are long, and we experience the summer months; when it's tilted away from the sun, the nights extend, and we endure winter. The longest and shortest days of the year are called the **solstices**, and the days in between, when our days and nights are of equal length, are called the **equinoxes**. Depending on your location, you might experience these occasions differently. For example, if you're close to the equator, you won't notice the days lengthening or shortening as much at the solstices, but you might notice a change in precipitation.

Although seasonal changes are subtle in some places, no matter where you are, different times of year have different qualities. Recall the *shi-meng* classification found in the Duke of Zhou's dream book (page 84).

We've been diving deeper into the creative and mystical aspects of dreaming. Notice whether this has any effect on the quality or content of your dreams themselves—and whether they, in turn, affect your connection to the spiritual in your waking life.

REFLECT:

Return to your dream journal, paying attention to dates. Notice whether the time of year had any effect on your dreaming. Do your journal entries reflect any seasonal themes or imagery? This could be bold and literal (leaves turning, snow falling, green grass growing under a bright sun) or more subtle and atmospheric (a theme of anticipation in spring, culmination at midsummer, harvest in late summer, or a sense of ancestral connection around Halloween or Día de los Muertos).

Pay particular attention to the dreams you have at the spokes of a year: the solstices, the equinoxes, and the cross-quarter days in between. Many cultures understand these days of alignment to carry spiritual potency.

PLAY:

Another calendar we cycle through each year is the **zodiac**—a system based on the stars and the constellations we've assigned them. If you're familiar with astrology, pay attention to the signs as we move through them each year, noticing any influence they may have on your dreaming life.

The watery sign of **Pisces** is the last sign in the cycle, closely associated with dreaming as well as death and endings. Pay particular attention to your dreams during Pisces season—roughly February 19 through March 20. What do you notice? Research your birth chart to discover whether you have any significant Piscean placements. Does your Sun, Moon, Mercury, Venus, Mars, or ascendant (your "rising sign") fall in Pisces? What might this mean for you?

Pisces is ruled by **Neptune**—the planet said to oversee our dreams. Because of its distance from the sun, Neptune has a much larger orbit than Earth and takes longer to move through the zodiac. While other planets shift between signs over weeks or months, Neptune remains in the same sign for more than twenty years at a time. Find an astrologer you trust and ask them to help you identify any notable **aspects** (angles) or **conjunctions** (alignments) Neptune has made with other planets this year. What were you dreaming about at the time? Or if such an event is upcoming, note it in your dream journal for later review.

What sign is Neptune in now? Where was it the year you were born?

SPOKES IN THE WHEEL

SPRING EQUINOX

March 20 in the Northern Hemisphere

September 20 in the Southern Hemisphere

BELTANE

May 1 in the Northern Hemisphere

November 1 in the Southern Hemisphere

SUMMER SOLSTICE

June 21 in the Northern Hemisphere

December 21 in the Southern Hemisphere

LUNASA

August 1 in the Northern Hemisphere

February 1 in the Southern Hemisphere

AUTUMN EQUINOX

September 20 in the Northern Hemisphere

March 20 in the Southern Hemisphere

SAMHAIN

October 31/November 1 in the Northern Hemisphere

April 30/May 1 in the Southern Hemisphere

WINTER SOLSTICE

December 21 in the Northern Hemisphere

June 21 in the Southern Hemisphere

IMBOLC

February 1 in the Northern Hemisphere

August 1 in the Southern Hemisphere

CHECK IN:

The nice thing about cycles is that they keep on turning, so if you've taken a pause, you can hop back in and be carried along all over again. Keep up with writing down at least one dream a week, or if you've fallen out of practice, jump back into the cycle, riding its continuous current.

DREAMING JOURNEY:
THE LANGUAGE OF DREAMS

The modern-day English word "dream" might come from the Danish word *drøm*, meaning "joy" or "noise," or from the German word *traum*, meaning "illusion" or "phantasm." It may also have a connection to the Norse word *draugr*, meaning "ghost." In Old English, "dream" meant something akin to music or merriment.

Even in terms of etymology, dreams are hard to trace, possessing ambiguity and duality right down to the root—on the one side, pleasure and happiness; on the other, something mysterious and potentially ominous.

DREAM WORDS FROM AROUND THE WORLD

In English, we have "pipe dream," "dreamboat," "In your dreams!" and "Dream on!" Other languages have their own terms and expressions related to sleep and dreams.

- When trying to recall the details of an elusive dream, you might give up and say, "*Träume sind Schäume!*" This German idiom translates to "dreams are foam."
- In Mandarin Chinese, you can wish someone 做个美梦 (*zuò ge měi mèng*), meaning "Have a beautiful dream!" However, if your well-wishes don't work, your friend might tell you the next morning, 目不交睫 (*mù bù jiāo jié*), which literally means, "The eyelashes do not come together"—indicating they couldn't sleep.
- In Italian, you can bid someone "*Sogni d'oro*," which translates to "dreams of gold"—similar to the English expression "Sweet dreams!"
- *Hypnopédie* is the French term for learning new things in your sleep.

The Yansi word ***ndoey*** *has two meanings: "dream" and "beard." Like the many hairs that form a beard, dreams are made up of individual elements that exist in the context of a larger whole.*

WHAT'S ON YOUR MIND?

The frequent daydreamer—with their "head in the clouds," as we say in English—is no stranger to this question, and in many languages, idiomatic expressions exist to answer it.

POLISH: *Myśleć o niebieskich migdałach.* (I'm thinking of blue almonds.)

SPANISH: *Pensando en pajaritos preñados.* (I'm thinking about pregnant birds.) Or *Pensando en la inmortalidad del cangrejo.* (I'm thinking about the immortality of the crab.)

FINNISH: *Istun ja mietin syntyjä syviä.* (I'm sitting and wondering about the world's early origins.)

ROMANIAN: *A se gândi la nemurirea sufletului.* (I'm thinking about the immortality of the soul.)

PORTUGUESE: *Pensando na morte da bezerra.* (I'm thinking about the calf's death.)

The Tupi-Guarani people of the Amazon River basin use a distinct grammar when retelling dreams: A specific verb tense is employed, and the marker "ra'ú" is used throughout the telling—in just about every sentence—to denote it's a dream.

DREAM-SPEAK

Sometimes people dream in languages they don't speak fluently but may have dabbled in years ago. One explanation for this is that a language we know well is stored on the left side of the brain, but the information we pick up when we're learning a new language is stored on the right side—the side associated with dreaming—perhaps making it more accessible to us while we're asleep.

Our brains store information in interesting ways; knowledge we may have forgotten or buried deep can surface unexpectedly in our dreams. Sometimes, though, our brains convince us we're dreaming in another language, when really we're just speaking gibberish.

CYCLE XII

DIVING DEEP

CYCLE XII WEEK 1 NEW MOON

CHILDHOOD DREAMS

Children need several more hours of sleep each night than adults, and they spend more of that time dreaming. Dreams from childhood are often particularly vivid, and some stick with us throughout our lives.

So much seems possible during childhood as we're figuring out how the world works and what we believe. Monsters take on real, terrifying forms, lurking in closets and under beds—perhaps representing the more abstract, emotional fears children experience.

REFLECT:

Think back as far as you can, to your very first memory. Write about it, recalling as many sensory details as possible. Try to reinhabit your perspective from that time; notice whether your consciousness feels different. Children's minds are impressionable; they're constantly taking in new stimuli, sorting and making sense of it all.

Though you have probably changed a lot since childhood, you are fundamentally the same person now as you were then, linked by a chain of dreams that has brought you here today.

What dreams do you remember from your childhood?

*The **Sandman** is a benevolent dream visitor from European folklore: a sock-footed old man who visits children and throws sand in their faces so they'll close their eyes and drift off to sleep. Once the children are quiet and still, the Sandman tells fantastical tales, entertaining them with sweet, colorful stories so they remain asleep.*

EXPLORE:

What were you afraid of as a child? Have you overcome those fears as an adult, or do they still linger for you?

Set a timer for five minutes and write a list of every fear you've ever had—as many as you can remember. This might feel a little scary at first; you may worry about conjuring the things you fear by writing them down, or even just by giving them space in your thoughts. But writing is a protected space, and this activity may even help you externalize your fears, minimizing their power over you.

After five minutes, put your pen down and review your list. Have your fears changed over the course of your life? Can you trace a sort of "lineage," noting how a particular fear has morphed over the years, manifesting in different forms?

PLAY:

Throughout this book, we've encouraged play and lightheartedness as a way to access deeper truths. This week, take that a step further by finding ways to invite childlike energy into your days. If you have children in your life, take time to play with them on their level. Try asking them to tell you about their dreams—or ask them where they think dreams come from!

If, as a child, you loved a particular activity or toy, get a little silly and relive that experience. Treat yourself to childlike delight: Scribble in a coloring book, barrel-roll down a hill, read a picture book, or visit the playground and swing or go down the slide.

CONJURE:

Plan to meet your child-self in your dreams. Find a photo of yourself at the age you wish to meet and gaze at it before bed. Try to remember what life was like at that time—what *you* were like and how you saw the world. Ask your dreams to reintroduce you to yourself.

Alternatively, ask your dreams to let you embody that age again.

You know the drill: Write your intention in your dream journal, meditate on it as you lie down, and fall asleep planning to meet your child-self—or to see the world through their eyes. In the morning, record your dream, reflecting on any messages you received.

Encountering your child-self, or attempting to inhabit their perspective, whether you do so in dreams or in a waking therapeutic space, can be quite healing, especially if you struggle with feelings of shame or self-loathing. By revisiting your foundation—your early years—with today's perspective, you might better understand context that can unlock insight into who you've become.

CYCLE XII WEEK 2 ◑ WAXING MOON

NIGHTMARES

Almost everyone has experienced a **nightmare**—a frightening or unpleasant dream that leaves a powerful emotional impression. Scary dreams are most common in childhood, and as we explored earlier this month, their memory can sometimes stay with us throughout our lives.

Nightmares are especially common after emotionally charged and traumatic experiences. They help our brains process the stress we've endured, giving us a chance to release some of it and move on. Our minds replay the event while our bodies are detached from the immediacy of the situation, diluting the emotion and allowing the experience to be worked through.

Nightmares can also arise out of physical stress, such as illness. Many people report having more vivid, disturbing dreams when they have a fever.

For those plagued by recurring nightmares, dreaming is not pleasurable, and sleep can become dreaded. People experiencing post-traumatic stress disorder (PTSD) frequently suffer from persistent, intense nightmares, and medical interventions, such as therapeutic counseling or medication, are often recommended.

Talk therapy, when available, has been shown to benefit people with recurrent nightmares. Additionally, sharing a nightmare with another person—even just with a loved one—has proven one of the most reliable ways to diminish its hold over the dreamer.

EXPLORE:

Pain and fear are not enjoyable sensations, and we generally want to avoid them. It may seem natural to forget about a nightmare or bad dream as soon as you wake up, pushing it away and hoping the uncomfortable feelings disappear. But what if the nightmare is trying to show you something you've been ignoring? Entertain the possibility that a nightmare can sometimes be a gift.

If this idea feels too challenging at the moment, it's OK to return to it later. However, do write down any nightmares you experience. You can revisit them when you're ready to explore why they may have surfaced.

PLAY:

One way to overcome a nightmare is to picture something that makes you feel good—a person who loves you, a beloved animal, a place of beauty, or a food or sensation you enjoy. If you wake in fear, counter it by visualizing the thing you love in your mind's eye, noticing its every detail. Let the warmth of your positive regard spread, replacing the horror of the bad dream.

Not every bad situation has a lesson, but many do. A nightmare will likely return as long as it has something to show you. The goal is to process it so it no longer has power over you, allowing you to move on.

CONSIDER:

Confronting our fears in a low-stakes dream setting, where any injury we incur does not physically wound, can boost our confidence. This newfound courage can then be carried into our waking lives, helping us face our real-life antagonists.

REFLECT:

Often, a single unpleasant emotion can linger in memory longer than hundreds of pleasant ones.

Can you remember any nightmares from before you began recording your dreams? Write an account of your most vivid one from memory, reflecting on any waking events, life circumstances, or emotions that may have coincided with the dream. What might the nightmare have been trying to tell you? Have you since moved on from its lesson or the event that triggered it—or has it returned more recently in a different form?

GO DEEPER

If you experience ongoing nightmares or stress dreams that negatively affect your waking life, or if the bad dreams have ceased to be helpful and are only causing annoyance, dismay, or unease, it may be time to turn to dreamwork, moving past the nightmare to regain a sense of control over your psyche.

Take these steps to address a persistent nightmare:

* **Upon waking, lie still**. Nightmares and stress dreams often jolt us awake into full alertness, and it can be difficult to fall back asleep immediately. By remaining still, we increase the chances of reentering the dream realm.
* **Establish a hypnagogic state.** Return to where you left off in your dream—but instead, drifting back into sleep and a more passive role, use your conscious mind to imagine a positive outcome.
* **Indulge in fantasy.** Imagine yourself a hero with magical abilities or powers that allow you to overcome the source of your torment. Visualize the twist it takes to get to a happy ending, no matter how far-fetched.

HINT: *If you can't remember the details of your dream, focus instead on the lingering emotion. Give shape to your feeling of fear or dread—perhaps it takes the form of a sleep demon or a monster. Imagine the monster in detail, but once you've conjured it, don't dwell on this part of the process. Instead, visualize yourself destroying it. Fight it, and win. Grow much larger than it, then walk away; or shrink it, stuffing it into a bottle or stomping on it so it can do no more harm. Hopefully, after vanquishing your adversary, you can drift into a more restful sleep.*

The Mara may have eyes of different colors, such as one blue and one green, or a unibrow, and she can transform into objects or animals at will, especially favoring moths.

Historically, people understood nightmares as curses brought on by demons. Many cultures describe entities that may be torturing the dreamer—mentally or sometimes physically.

* The **Divs** are large, monstrous demons featured in Persian folklore. Commonly depicted with claws, horns, and long, tusklike teeth, Divs possess the dreamlike ability to shape-shift. They do the opposite of what anyone asks or tells them to do, which is perhaps why they sleep during the day and come out at night. According to some legends, Divs used to reign over Earth, causing chaos, but they were defeated by heroes and banished, returning only to haunt humans while they sleep.

* In European folklore, the **Mara**, whose name is echoed in the word "nightmare," is a woman who slips into bedrooms through the keyhole. She sits on a dreamer's chest, paralyzing them and inducing terrifying dreams. The Mara can appear as either a beautiful woman or a hideous hag. As a **succubus**, she haunts the night, bringing terror and devouring souls while people sleep.

* A **Nocnitsa**, similar to the Mara, is a female spirit in Slavic mythology that comes to torment people while they sleep. A Nocnitsa is made of shadows, and her voice is a piercing wail. She smells like moss and dirt, and her scent can enter your dreams and linger in your room long after her visit.

CYCLE XII WEEK 3 FULL MOON

DREAMING THE DEAD

In Homer's *The Iliad*, the famous Greek war hero Achilles is visited in a dream by his beloved friend Patroclus after Patroclus's death in battle. Patroclus tells Achilles that he must perform the proper burial rites for him. In his grief, Achilles tries to touch and hold his friend one last time but instead wakes in despair over his loss. However, the dream prompts him to carry out the funereal ritual, which allows Patroclus to move on and Achilles to find some closure.

The loss of a loved one through death is one of the most intense and challenging experiences a person can endure. When a deceased loved one—or even an acquaintance who has passed—appears in a dream, it can be unsettling. For a night, it feels as though they never left this plane of existence.

The way the dead appear in dreams can vary: They might seem youthful, happy, or troubled; they might appear as you remember them, or quite different—perhaps even in a new physical form.

REFLECT:

Before bed, write a letter in your dream journal to someone you've lost, especially if you have unresolved emotions surrounding their departure. Try writing your message as if their spirit is present with you. Express what you wish you could say to them, and include any questions you'd like them to answer.

CONSIDER:

Dreaming and the Underworld have long been linked due to their shared dark, amorphous atmospheres—where things are not what they seem—and their primal, immaterial intensity. We have limited access to these realms; both are planes of mystery to the living. But are they one and the same or just neighboring territories?

In some cultures, it is taken for granted that when a deceased loved one visits in a dream, it's their spirit returning. Other cultures interpret this as the mind's way of psychologically processing grief. One explanation comes from within, the other from outside the individual. Dreams can sometimes alter our very worldviews and understanding of life, death, the in-between, and the beyond.

PLAY:

If you haven't done so before, consider researching your ancestry. Gather information about the blood relatives who came before you—or if that isn't accessible, think of the concept of "ancestor" more broadly. Perhaps you're aware of a geographic region you descend from; maybe there's a historical figure you sense a connection with; or perhaps you travel even further into the evolutionary past, getting to know an animal ancestor.

If you're looking into your blood lineage, ask relatives for photos; seek out objects, heirlooms, or writings connected to your ancestors. If you can, bring one of these to your dream altar.

Whether you're exploring your biological heritage or something more figurative, reflect on the fact that a long line of people overcame great struggles—bore and raised children or gave birth in other ways—to make way for your existence. Those people also dreamt every night, and many of them may have revered the power of their dreams.

If it feels safe and comfortable, try inviting specific ancestors—biological or spiritual—to visit you in your dreams this week.

EXPLORE:

Loss is inevitable, and each of us carries with us some form of grief. Yet in our modern world, we often lack supportive or easily accessible ways to process this grief. Sitting with or talking about the experience can be helpful—and our dreams are a common, free, and universal way to come to better terms with loss.

When a departed loved one visits in a dream, be gentle with yourself in the days to follow. These experiences can be sweet and loving, but they may also be earthshaking and unpredictable, and in some cases, overwhelmingly sad or scary.

Is it possible that your loved one is seeking your help with some unfinished business? Are you willing to lend a hand? If the request is one you can reasonably fulfill, like Patroclus's request of Achilles, you might choose to honor it as a way of seeking closure. On the other hand, it might represent an emotional or psychological need of your own. Reflect on what the dream might reveal about your own feelings.

SPIRITUALISM

In the early twentieth century, **Spiritualists** believed that responses from séances and automatic writing (see page 91) were messages from supernatural entities and that practitioners could act as mediums to channel the voices of the dead. The telephone was still a relatively new and groundbreaking technology—suddenly people could communicate with the disembodied voices of their loved ones far away in real time. This once-unimaginable possibility opened up new horizons: If communicating with distant friends and family was now possible, why not communicate with the dead?

Note: If you've never had a dream visitation from a deceased loved one, that's nothing to worry about. It doesn't mean that your loved one doesn't care for you or that you've let their memory fade.

CHECK IN:

Communing with—or even just attempting to commune with—lost loved ones or ancestors can be deeply emotional and may take a toll in your waking life. Go easy on yourself, and seek support as you need it. Share your reflections with those you trust, and balance the challenges of this week with simple measures of self-care:
Stay hydrated, spend time outdoors, and make an effort to connect with community.

CYCLE XII WEEK 4 WANING MOON

THE WATER CONNECTION

Poetically, metaphysically, and symbolically, dreams and emotions have a strong relationship with water—its fluidity and mutability, its flow and depths. In tarot, the suit of Cups (often depicted as liquid-filled chalices, goblets, or bowls) represents matters of the heart and intuition.

Falling asleep can feel like entering a body of water: Sometimes you wade in slowly; other nights it's a sudden plunge. And like bodies of water, the depth of dreams can vary. Our perspective might change the deeper we go, and we may encounter stranger creatures in the deepest depths.

THE DEEP WELL OF THE SUBCONSCIOUS

Dreams do us the great favor of surfacing insight without our conscious effort; they can reveal feelings in our lives that we may not be consciously aware of yet. For example, you might dream of kissing someone you've met only once, because your body senses an attraction your mind has ignored or denied. (Though, of course, there may be other, symbolic explanations for this kind of dream!) Medically, there have been many cases of people dreaming about an illness before they were diagnosed or even aware of being ill; this may be because our bodies detect an imbalance before our minds recognize it.

CONSIDER:

Reflect on different bodies and states of water. What emotions do you associate with each form? For example, imagine the emotional qualities of a tidal wave; a soft, gentle rain; a plume of steam; a waterfall; or a frozen pond. You can also try this in reverse, starting with emotions like grief, joy, fear, boredom, or anticipation, imagining each as a type or form of water.

PLAY:

Sip into and out of sleep.

Before bed, fill a glass of water. Thank the water and tell it your dream intention for the night. Drink from it, then leave it on your bedside table as you drift off to sleep.

HINT: *If you have cats who might try to drink from your water overnight, place a light book or other makeshift lid over the top of the glass.*

First thing in the morning, drink from the glass again, providing a sense of continuity between states. Then write down your dream or reflections.

REFLECT:

Revisit your journal and notice when water has appeared in your dreams. Ask yourself:

What form did the water take? How did it move? How did I engage with it? Was there any other kind of life interacting with or moving through it?

Water dreams can offer insight into our emotions and how we're processing them—whether we're actively working through them or avoiding doing so. Dreams of drowning, for example, are to be heeded as warnings, typically signaling emotional overwhelm. In general, flowing water tends to represent a healthier relationship to emotions than stagnant or frozen water, but gushing water might indicate a loss of emotional control.

Dreams flow like water, helping us flush out what we can't use and keeping us fresh and healthy as life's stream drifts onward. In this way, dreams help us process and heal.

In ancient Ireland, poets and magicians were one and the same, and they would receive inspiration by sitting near bodies of water.

EXPLORE:

Sit by the edge of a body of water: a pond, lake, river, sea, swimming pool—or even a bathtub. If you can, enter the water, briefly submerging yourself. At the very least, dip in your toes or splash water on your face. Pay attention to how this element feels against your skin. Notice its qualities: its movement or stillness, its clarity or murkiness, its temperature. As you meditate in or near the water, try to internalize some of those qualities, inviting them into your dreams this week.

DREAMING JOURNEY:
GODS AND SPIRITS

MESOPOTAMIAN DREAM SPIRITS

Alû is a spirit with no mouth or ears who enjoys frightening people in their dreams by lying across them like a blanket; his victims become hot, and their ears start to ring as they enter a coma-like state.

* **Mamu** and **Sisig**, the daughter and son of **Utu**, the Mesopotamian sun god, rule the dream realm together. They also represent aspects of the human soul. Sisig is a **psychopomp**—a divine guide who leads souls between dimensions, whether to the dream realm or the realm of the dead. Mamu's dreams are oracular, capable of predicting and influencing the future. Because we each contain the spirits of Sisig and Mamu within us, we are able to access their gifts while we sleep.

* **Nanshe** is the goddess of prophecy, bringing oracular messages to people through dreams. She is also the goddess of social welfare and a caretaker of nature, with a fondness for vulnerable people like widows and orphans; her messages tend to be political in nature. She is often depicted with geese.

ANCIENT GREEK GODS OF DREAMING

A small pantheon of Greek gods reigned over the realm of sleep and dreaming.

First, there are the old gods, the ancient ones: **Erebus**, god of darkness, and his partner **Nyx**, goddess of night. They are brother and sister, born of the primordial god **Chaos**, and together they had twin sons: **Thanatos**, the god of peaceful death, and **Hypnos**, the god of sleep. Hypnos met his match in **Pasithea**, the goddess of rest and relaxation. Hypnos and Pasithea had several children together, collectively known as the **oneiroi**: the dark-winged bringers of dreams.

Morpheus is the leader of the oneiroi, said to shape dreams. He appears to dreamers in the form of people they know and delivers messages they need to hear. One of his brothers, **Phobetor**, brings nightmares, and another, **Phantasos**, brings dreams of bright, bizarre fantasy. By some accounts, there are one thousand oneroi, each delivering a particular kind of dream. These gods and goddesses of the night-realm live in a poppy-filled cave beyond the reach of the sun. The oneiroi emerge each night like a flock of bats, passing through two pillars: one of horn, and one of ivory—that is, one of true prophecy and one of meaningless illusion.

ANCIENT EGYPTIAN DREAM DEITIES

* **Bes** protects households from bad dreams, especially the children who reside there. He's depicted as a stout, naked dwarf, and unlike most representations of Egyptian gods, he faces the world head-on, not in profile. He scares off evil and represents all the joyful things in life: music, humor, sex, dance, festivity. If a baby laughs for no reason, it's because Bes is making faces at them. No wonder he was one of the most popular gods of the time!

* **Tutu** stands guard against bad dreams with the head of a man, the body of a lion, a snake for a tail, and hawk and crocodile heads growing from his shoulders. People made small personal shrines for Tutu inside their homes to ward off nightmares, with offerings of goose meat and bread to show their gratitude.

OTHER DREAM ENTITIES FROM AROUND THE GLOBE

* In Japan, the **Baku** is a colorful, dragon-like creature with a long snout that visits dreamers' houses at night and snorts up nightmares. According to legend, the gods created the Baku from leftover scraps after making all the other creatures of the world. If you want the Baku to protect you, you must draw it before you fall asleep. However, caution is advised when summoning the Baku: If called upon too often, it may tire of eating nightmares and instead gobble up hopes and memories.

* **The Batibat** is a fat female spirit from the Philippines who lives peacefully in trees. However, if her tree home is chopped down, she will haunt the location where it stood, seeking revenge on anyone who sleeps there by suffocating them at night and haunting them throughout the day. To escape this around-the-clock nightmare, one must bite their thumb or wiggle their toes—small physical actions that can, in fact, stir one out of sleep paralysis. Surviving the Batibat is said to allow one the ability to see spirits that others cannot ever after.

* **Caer Ibormeith** is the Celtic goddess of dreams. She alternates between human and swan forms, transforming on Samhain. In one story, she repeatedly visited **Aengus**, the god of love, in his dream, and he became enamored of her. To be with her outside of his dreams, however, Aengus would have to recognize her in swan form. He turned himself into a swan and was able to identify her among a large flock. Swans and geese are meaningful symbols in the dream realm, as they can traverse land, water, and air, moving through realms with ease. It is said you can call on Caer Ibormeith if you desire a prophetic dream, especially one about love.

* **Household spirits** exist in the folklore of many cultures worldwide: the **Brownie** in Anglo-Scottish tales; the **Domovoi** in Slavic stories; the **Duende** in Spanish folklore; the **Gasin** in Korean legends; the **Lutin** in French tales; and the **Nisse**, **Tonttu**, or **Tomte** in Nordic stories. While some details vary, the general concept is similar: These protective spirits dwell in our homes with us, though they are adept at hiding and largely go unseen. Although sightings are rare, they are often likened to goblins or gnomes, are described

as small and wizened, sometimes hairy, and usually wear a hat. They come out at night to make mischief, "borrow" things, or—if we're lucky—help with chores. If you're on their good side (maybe you take good care of your home, or maybe you've left them offerings of flowers or food), they may appear in your dreams with solutions to your troubles, with warnings, or to reveal hidden treasure. If they're displeased, however, they might disturb your sleep by breaking things or pinching you.

* **Hine-nui-te-pō** is a Maori goddess from New Zealand whose name translates to "Great Woman of the Night." She takes in the spirits of the dead, escorting them to her kingdom of Night. She is responsible for the rich red colors of the sunset.

* **Morana**, or **Marzanna**, is a Slavic pagan goddess of sorcery and winter, also associated with sleep, dreams, renewal, and rebirth. At the end of each winter, Marzanna is ceremonially drowned to make way for the goddess of spring. To this day, on the Spring Equinox, people make effigy dolls of Marzanna out of twigs and grasses and toss her into a body of water in a ritual to welcome new beginnings.

CATHOLIC SAINTS

While not deities or even spirits exactly, Catholic saints are believed to be responsible for miracles (at least two are required for official sainthood). The Catholic faithful can petition these saints to intercede on their behalf, often within specific realms, including those of dreams and sleep.

* **Saint Hildegard von Bingen (1098–1179)** was a German Benedictine abbess, composer, and philosopher. One of the few women named a "Doctor of the Church" for her intellectual and artistic contributions, she is the patron saint of writing, music, and—according to some sources—dreams. From a young age, Hildegard suffered from migraines that caused visual auras, and she received visions she believed came from God, which she used to compose music, compile herbariums, and invent her own language.

* **Saint Catherine of Bologna (1413–1463)** was an Italian nun as well as a writer and painter. She is the patron saint of artists and the imagination, which goes hand in hand with dreams, especially if you're looking to your dreams for creative inspiration. Catherine herself experienced dreams and visions that inspired her artwork.

Bon voyage!

CONCLUDING YOUR JOURNEY

When a dream ends, it's because you wake up. When a day ends, you enter a new dream. Nothing is gone—everything is change.

Dreaming and waking are two sides of the same coin, existing side by side and making up the whole of human life. Appreciating the unique qualities of each can help us find a healthy balance as we travel back and forth between the two realms. Ideally, we participate fully in both, deepening our connection to the cosmos during our fleeting time on Earth. We don't use dreams as an escape, nor do we deny their value. We keep the channels open so we can flow through these realms with ease while recognizing their differences.

FINAL REFLECTIONS

By now, you probably have a notebook (or more than one!) filled with dreams. Take some time to read them, remember them, and appreciate what they've offered. Reflect on how they've enriched your waking life, deepening and expanding your reality. Do you have any favorite dreams? Are there any outstanding riddles they've posed? Take a step back and consider your dream journal as a whole. Notice any major or recurring themes, meanings, or messages.

If you're so inclined, open to a new page, and spend some time journaling in response to these prompts, thinking back over the past year of dreamwork:

* WHAT HAVE YOU LEARNED? Consider what knowledge you've gained about yourself, about dreaming, or about life in general.
* HOW HAVE YOU CHANGED? Reflect on any shift thats in your perspective or beliefs, your habits or patterns.
* WHERE WILL YOU GO FROM HERE? If you plan to continue your dreamwork, identify any exercises you may wish to repeat, perhaps amending or expanding them. List any new topics or techniques you'd like to explore next.

Finally, thank yourself for staying the course! You've honored your dreams by giving them attention and care—a rare thing in modern society.

CELEBRATE!

TAKE SOME TIME TO BASK IN YOUR ACCOMPLISHMENT.

Bake a dream cake. Throw a party. Share some of the writing or artwork you've produced, or create something new to mark this occasion. Find some way to commemorate your journey!

As dreams often show, within every ending is a new beginning. While you're closing out this chapter of the journey, you're also returning to where it began. With the wisdom you've gained from your travels, you may have earned a deeper appreciation for "home"—where you are now in life.

Remember, that this book is an atlas, a map you can revisit as often as you like, plotting a different course with each voyage. And whether or not you return, your dreams will always remain available to you: a constant source of guidance.

When you're ready, you can raise that sail again and set out toward a new horizon.

BLUE MOON

COLLABORATIVE DREAMING

Dreaming is one of the most personal and private experiences we can have: Our secret wishes, fears, memories, vanities, and weaknesses are laid bare each night for our eyes only. We fall asleep, and elaborate stories unfold—full of dilemmas, temptations, private successes, and bizarre, colorful events.

However, in some cultures, dreams are seen as having collaborative potential; they represent a fertile spiritual landscape where individuals can come together. By dedicating shared time and attention to the dream realm while awake, people can strengthen their bonds and connect to a, power beyond themselves.

If you wish to go further, the final portion of this book offers a series of nightly challenges to try with a partner or group. To get the most out of these experiments, engage in them with people you trust. This undertaking will likely encroach on some personal, vulnerable territory, so it can be a powerful way to deepen relationships.

How seriously you and your partner(s) wish to take this work is up to you. You might want to keep it fun and playful, or you might engage with more intensity. Any approach is welcome, so long as it's mutually agreed upon.

Keep in mind that not everyone enjoys hearing about others' dreams; in fact, some people find it distinctly irritating or boring! Be sure your dream partners are as invested and interested in these exercises as you are—preferably, they've already completed meaningful dreamwork on their own.

This short guide offers suggestions for getting started and several exercises to deepen your collaboration. You might sprinkle these activities throughout one lunar month—a thirteenth moon or "blue moon," if you like—or spread them over a much longer period. Find a pace that feels comfortable for all involved.

CHOOSE AND INTERVIEW YOUR DREAM PARTNER

Select a companion you trust: a friend, spouse, partner, or sibling. You can try these experiments across distances or while sharing the same room or bed; notice whether there's any difference.

To understand each other on a dream level, begin by conducting dream interviews. Below are some sample questions to guide you, but feel free to add your own, and skip over any you can't or don't want to answer. The interview can take place in person, over the phone or via video, or through written communication. Take as long as you need to complete this step—at least two days, devoting one day to each partner's responses.

MOTIVATIONS

- Why did you first embark on dreamwork?
- What do you hope to get out of collaborative dreamwork? How do you expect it will differ from solo work?

EXPERIENCES

- What is dreaming like for you? (What does it look like? What does it feel like?)
- What important lessons have you drawn from earlier dreamwork?
- Tell me about a dream so vivid it's stuck with you for a long time. What's the earliest dream you remember having?
- Referring to the *Plotting Discoveries* list on page xiv, what are some interesting dream experiences you've had? Have you ever had a Big Dream?
- Are there any recurring elements—themes, people, places, objects, etc.—in your dreams?

BELIEFS

- Do you have any cultural, religious, or familial connections that inform your philosophy of dreaming?
- What about personal dream theories (e.g., why we dream, where dreams come from, or how we can use them)?

CREATIVITY

- Share one of your favorite dream journal entries from the past year.
- Have you produced any artwork based on your dreams? Are you willing to share it?

LAY A SUPPORTIVE FRAMEWORK

Once you've interviewed one another about your dreaming histories, shift the conversation to the present. Establish how you'd like to communicate moving forward. Ideally, you'll check in with each other regularly (at least weekly) to report your dreams.

Maybe you'll send each other morning texts containing a few dream keywords. Perhaps you'll type your journal entries and email them, or text photos of handwritten journal pages. For real-time connection, you can relate your dreams over the phone or via video, or schedule dates to meet in person. Of course, if you share a bed with your dream partner, you might just roll over and exchange dreams when you first wake up.

However you choose to communicate, take turns, alternating who goes first, and agree that when one partner is sharing, the other will listen attentively.

ESTABLISH PARAMETERS

Name your own needs and listen to your partner's—then synthesize them into an agreed-upon list of ground rules you'll both follow. Here are a few you might consider:

* Keep dream reports and discussion confidential, sharing only with explicit permission.
* Remain open-minded and avoid judgment.
* Understand that your partner isn't responsible for what they dream about. If what they share triggers a negative or uncomfortable emotional response in you, communicate openly so you can discuss it, and take a break if needed.

CULTIVATE A REGULAR EXCHANGE

Abiding by the expectations you've agreed to with your partner, begin sharing your dreams regularly. Both of you can share every week, or you can alternate weeks—your turn this week, theirs next week, and so forth. If you're sharing orally, meeting in person or over the phone, you might consider offering an initial account of your dream, then retelling it after a pause. Sometimes this repetition can help more details emerge.

Offer to share interpretive insights with each other. You may find it's easier to decode your partner's dreams than your own. Often, meaning will arise intuitively, but you can also return to the symbol interpretation (page 66) or dream decoding exercises (page 18) on your partner's behalf, seeing if some distance provides new clues.

HINT: *Pay attention to any similarities, common themes, or coincidences your dreams share. Speak these observations aloud.*

THE MAIMONIDES DREAM LAB

The mid-twentieth century was a time of heightened curiosity around **psychic phenomena** or "psi," resulting in greater funding for research on the mind, consciousness, and telepathy. From 1964 until 1978, Maimonides Hospital in Brooklyn, New York, housed a well-funded dream laboratory where scientists tested the boundaries of the unknown and the irrational.

In one experiment, a telepathic sender ("agent") met briefly with a telepathic receiver ("subject") at the Dream Lab before the two entered separate rooms for the night. The subject was hooked up to electrodes, with EEG machines monitoring their brain waves while they slept. When the subject's sleep cycle began, a buzzer sounded in the agent's room, cuing them to focus mental energy on a randomly selected photograph or art print, in an attempt to transmit the image to the subject's mind. As soon as the subject's eyelids began to flutter, indicating REM sleep, they were awakened and questioned about any dreams. This was done throughout the night, a different image transmitted with each sleep cycle.

The results were interesting! In many cases, the dreamers' reports closely matched the target image. Although these findings were met with considerable skepticism and critique, they remain an influential part of the history of dream research.

DREAM TELEPATHY

After you've been sharing with your dream partner for a few days or weeks—however long it takes to establish a comfortable rhythm—you can experiment with **dream telepathy**: the transmission of information from one mind to another through dreams.

The idea here is that thoughts are things, and they can be sent and shared across space and time. Anyone who's ever had an idea come out of "nowhere"—inspiration, a muse—knows this can be quite a mysterious and uncanny phenomenon. According to dream researcher **Stanley Krippner**, emotional thoughts are the most powerful and therefore the most easily transmittable—hence why people sometimes report experiencing a loved one's pain or distress in their dreams.

Try a version of the Maimonides experiment with your dream partner, taking turns as "agent" and "subject." Although you won't be able to pinpoint the *exact* moment when you or your partner enters REM sleep, you can approximate it.

CHOOSE YOUR ROLES. Who will be the agent and who will be the subject?

AGREE ON A BEDTIME. The subject tells the agent what time they plan to fall asleep. As the subject gets ready for bed, they should set an alarm for ninety minutes after the agreed-upon time—so they'll likely be awakened while in their first REM phase, and more likely to remember what they're experiencing.

HINT: *If your dream partner is long-distance, watch out for time zones!*

SELECT AN IMAGE TO TRANSMIT. Meanwhile, the agent should choose a vibrant yet simple painting, drawing, or photograph to focus on at the designated bedtime, staring intently at the image and concentrating on "sending" it to their dream partner.

DOCUMENT THE DREAM. When the subject wakes to their alarm, they should write down their dream in as much detail as possible. Later, they will read or send what they've written to the agent.

NOTICE ANY SIMILARITIES. If you're the agent, did your partner pick up on anything from the image you chose? Perhaps there's a detail, color scheme, or mood that appears in both the image and their dream. Feel free to try this multiple times, switching roles as you wish, and see if your skills improve.

ARRANGE A MEETING IN THE DREAM REALM

Using the framework of the dream telepathy experiment, play with visiting each other in your dreams. To give your visit more shape and purpose, decide who will be the visitor and who will be the host.

The first time you intentionally plan to meet in a dream together, choose to meet somewhere you've both been in real life, whether it's something generic, like "a cafe" or "the beach," or a specific place, like "Aunt Jessie's attic."

There are online communities where people collaboratively create entire dream universes. For example, if one person dreams about a lighthouse and shares it with the group, it becomes a collective goal for others to find that lighthouse in their dreams. Together, they build and explore whole worlds.

ANNOUNCE YOUR INTENTION. Before bed, the visitor says: "I am going to visit [host's name] in my dream tonight." Meanwhile, the host will say: "[Visitor's name] will visit me in my dreams tonight."

RECORD AND COMPARE NOTES. In the morning, record your dreams, sharing them with one another. Did either of you see the other? Did you share any common experiences, emotions, or settings? Or were your dreams parallel in some other way? Celebrate any coincidences, and see if you can build on them!

BOUNDARIES AND COMMUNICATION

Sometimes in dreams we can feel what others feel, or experience emotions in new ways. As we discussed in Cycle VI, Week 1, boundaries are more fluid in dreams, and it might seem like we're channeling or even processing someone else's emotions in visceral, empathic ways.

But remember, any understanding we gain through dreams, imagination, and projection is no substitute for asking questions and listening to others share their truths, triumphs, and struggles in real life. We might receive hints or grains of insight, but none of us can truly read minds.

So communicate with your dream partner. If something isn't working—even if you're not exactly sure what, or why—tell them. If they express something similar to you, don't take it personally, and respect that this can be challenging work. Listen; pay attention to nonverbal cues; name observations aloud. Above all, be sensitive—both with yourself and your partner.

INTERPRET YOUR PARTNER'S DREAM ARTISTICALLY

Instead of decoding your partner's dream for meaning, look to it for creative inspiration. Exchange dream journal entries. Read your partner's dream, sit with it, then use one of the techniques discussed in Cycle VII—automatic drawing, collage, assemblage, dance, etc.—to capture it artistically.

Alternatively, let your partner's dream inspire a poem—a haiku, rhyming couplet, free-verse poem, prose poem, or whatever other form you're drawn to.

Once you've created something in response to your partner's dream, share it with them by presenting it as a gift. If you're both interested in this activity, you can do it regularly, trying out different dreams.

HINT: *To shake things up, try trading dream rituals one night, performing your partner's instead of your own.*

INCUBATE A DREAM COLLABORATIVELY

Tonight, before you go to sleep, settle on something you and your collaborator will both try to conjure in your dreams. As we explored in Cycle VI, Week 4, you can set an intention before bed to dream about something in particular, with the hope that it will make some kind of appearance.

CHOOSE AN OBJECT TO CONJURE. Start small, selecting something specific that both you and your partner have at home—like a coin or a certain book—to focus on. Alternatively, you can agree to seek out a particular object, like a rose, and bring it home to work with.

Refer to the Dream Incubation instructions on page 82 if needed.

RECORD YOUR DREAM. The next morning, write down your dream in as much detail as you can.

Note: This is not about testing each other or proving anything; it's simply about experimenting and seeing what happens.

REPORT BACK. Did either you or your dream partner encounter the object—and if so, where? In what context? Compare notes; sift carefully through your dreams and look for any overlaps. This is a time for hypothesis, so keep an open mind and have fun. Does it work better if you aim for something more poetic or abstract—incubating a dream about an archetype, say, or a color, or an emotion?

When two people dream together, the dream's power grows.

EXCHANGE DREAM RECIPES

Dream recipes, not unlike the "dream spells" we played with in Cycle XI, Week 3, are fanciful instructions for incubating specific dreams. Like cooking, dreaming is a form of alchemy, transforming one thing into another.

Try creating a dream recipe of your own! Is there a certain feeling or mood you'd like to invoke with your recipe (romantic, adventurous, exciting, soothing)? Or do you have a specific circumstance or setting in mind?

Note: You don't necessarily have to try your recipes or even ensure they're feasible in the waking world—perhaps you'll follow them in your dreams instead.

Adapt your dream spell to share with your partner. Write it on a recipe card and mail it to them.

DREAM KITCHEN

Leonora Carrington and **Remedios Varo** were Surrealist artists and best friends. Leonora, born in England in 1917, and Remedios, born in Spain in 1908, were drawn to Paris by their artistic talents and temperaments, becoming part of the avant-garde art scene. When the Nazi regime intensified its attacks in France, the two women independently fled to Mexico, where their friendship truly blossomed. They inspired each other through conversations about craft, feminism, esotericism, and dreams, among other things.

As multidisciplinary artists, they evoked feeling and provoked thought through language as well as with brush and paint. Known for their mischievous and "witchy" personas, they often pranked each other and came up with bizarre recipes to incubate specific dreams. These recipes were whimsical and playful, even as they explored the far reaches of consciousness.

GUIDED MEDITATIONS

Create a relaxing guided meditation experience for your companion. There are many recorded meditations available online that you can consult as examples, but feel free to innovate. This exercise works best when you both have at least an hour to spend together, either in person or over the phone, and it requires some preparation.

Take turns: On another night, your partner will create a soothing meditation for you.

PREPARE THE ENVIRONMENT. If you're delivering this meditation in person, you might light a candle or incense and play some gentle music or soothing nature sounds.

INVITE YOUR PARTNER TO LIE DOWN, placing a soft cloth or silken cover over their eyes, if they wish. Ensure that the room is dimly lit.

CAST A SPELL WITH YOUR WORDS, speaking calmly and slowly. Here is a prompt to help get you started:

> Let your body relax and feel heavy. Feel it supported by the ground. Take a deep breath in, then slowly breathe out. [Pause.] You are lying in [a beautiful place]. You feel [describe the temperature, the air, pleasant emotions]. You can smell [describe pleasant aromas: grass, flowers, earth]. You slowly stand up and decide to explore your surroundings. You see . . .

Or you could simply read this meditation aloud:

> You are in a forest. Rays of light shine through the trees' upper branches, casting dappled shadow on the ground. Birds sing around you: beautiful, gentle calls back and forth. Curious, you decide to go deeper into the woods. The path beneath your feet is soft, cushioning your bare feet. Moss grows up the tall, old trees. You reach out and touch one. Its trunk is warm, the bark rough against your fingertips. You smell the earthiness of the woods. You see your hand touching the tree. A gentle breeze moves across your skin. You feel the sun warming your hair. You walk deeper into the woods. You feel the life in the trees around you. You take your steps slowly. The trees are like tall beings surrounding you. You feel the wisdom they hold. You feel how ancient they are. You take a deep breath in, and you feel the trees around you moving, breathing, and growing. Their roots stretch out underground, beneath your feet; their branches reach into the air above you, interlacing and connected. Their leaves protect and shelter you. These trees are your ancestors, and they have a message for you. You are ready to listen and absorb their wisdom.

INVITE YOUR PARTNER BACK TO AWARENESS. After a few minutes of quiet, gently guide your partner out of their dreamlike state with your voice, or by ringing a bell or chime. Make sure your partner knows they're welcome to share anything about their experience with you, but they don't have to. Offer them a glass of water to drink, and if you lit a candle, blow it out to conclude the meditation.

TAPPING INTO THE ZEITGEIST

During the COVID-19 pandemic, dream researcher **Deirdre Barrett** conducted an international survey to investigate how dreams changed during this period of illness, anxiety, and isolation. Perhaps unsurprisingly, her findings revealed that people's sleep quality deteriorated, and their dreams became notably more vivid, with a significant increase in nightmares and stress dreams. Health care workers reported dreaming of the virus itself, reliving their daily efforts to treat it. By contrast, those sheltering at home experienced more metaphorical dreams: Some dreamed of being invaded by swarms of bugs and other vermin.

Similarly, after the September 11 attacks in New York City, many people reported that their dreams were affected by the event. Those who were present in the city during the attacks relived the experience in their dreams, while people who watched it on TV—less directly impacted—dreamed about other sorts of disasters, such as tsunamis and earthquakes, their dreams more symbolic in nature.

FORM A DREAM-SHARING CIRCLE

The 1970s saw a surge in group dreamwork, with many scholars and therapists studying dreams, leading workshops, forming dream groups, and releasing books about their methods and findings. The renewed interest in dreams spread beyond psychotherapy, gaining popularity among the general public.

One way both professionals and amateurs shared dreams was through dream circles, where participants gathered to share dreams and tap into the communal wisdom found in many cultures.

Gathering like-minded friends is indeed a powerful way to deepen your exploration of the dream realm and expand your personal dreamwork. You can start your own dream circle with your partner by reaching out to friends and interested parties, or you might look online for established dream-sharing groups in your area.

If you're starting a dream-sharing group of your own, here is how a session might look:

* **FORM A CIRCLE.** Sit so everyone can see each other.

* **BEGIN SHARING.** Ask for a volunteer to go first and allow them to speak uninterrupted as they share their dream.

* **INVITE RESPONSE.** When the dreamer is finished telling their dream, others can ask questions, point out any associations they notice, or relay what stands out. The dreamer, in turn, can share any connections they found relevant.

* **CONTINUE AROUND THE CIRCLE.** Move on to the next person, repeating the process. Note that not everyone will have the opportunity to share in every session.

Will you meet indoors? In a grassy park? What time will you meet—evening or midday? Consider how your decisions about when and where you meet may affect the experience.

GUIDING PRINCIPLES

Group dreamwork requires agreements, trust, and mutual respect. Just as you did your dream partnership, you'll want to enter into group dreamwork with a healthy awareness of your own boundaries and a willingness to respect those of others. Before joining or founding a group, consider these elements:

* **GROUP SIZE:** The ideal dream group is between four and ten people.
* **GROUND RULES:** If you're establishing a group rather than joining one, begin by agreeing on ground rules so members feel safe and respected when sharing potentially vulnerable dream experiences.
* **STRUCTURE:** These groups work best in a horizontal, nonhierarchical structure, without one leader making all the decisions. Be aware of power dynamics, including your own role in the circle. Rotate roles and responsibilities, especially if you choose to designate a facilitator for each session.
* **PURPOSE:** Group dreamwork is for personal growth and is not a replacement for clinical therapy. While there will inevitably be some overlap, remember that you are not working with professionals. You are the authority of your own life, and while others can offer new insights and perspectives, you must temper any advice with your own wisdom.

SURREALIST PARLOR GAMES

The Surrealists were fascinated by the dream realm and the creative possibilities it unlocked. They admired the way children behave without the constraints of convention and self-consciousness, and recognized how dreams could similarly liberate adults. Combining these interests, they invented games to create art collaboratively, later publishing their work in collectively run magazines.

QUESTIONS

The game of Questions offers a shortcut to the surreal, the unexpected, and often, a good laugh.

CUT A SHEET OF PAPER INTO SEVERAL STRIPS. Pile the strips on a dining-room or coffee table—wherever folks are gathered—or hand them out.

WRITE RANDOM QUESTIONS. Invite everyone to write a question on one of the strips: genuine queries, nonsense questions, poetic inquiries, mundane ones, or whatever comes up.

FOLD THE STRIPS. When everyone is finished writing, fold all the strips in half and toss them into a hat.

DRAW FROM THE HAT. Instruct everyone to draw a folded strip from the hat and, opening it to the blank side (avoiding seeing the question opposite), write the first thing that comes to mind—preferably in the form of a statement.

When all the strips have been written on, front and back, unfold them, taking turns reading both question and response aloud.

CONDITIONALS

This game is much like Questions and will largely follow the same steps.

Start by cutting and distributing strips of paper, this time inviting everyone to write the first half of a conditional statement (the "if" portion of an "if/then statement") on one of the strips.

"IF . . ."

Have them fold their strip and toss it into the hat. Once all strips are collected, have everyone draw one, and without peeking at the "if" already written, finish the conditional.

"THEN . . ."

Once again, go around the room, inviting everyone to read their complete "if/then" statement aloud.

EXQUISITE CORPSE

The Surrealists' best-known game, Exquisite Corpse, doesn't require words, so it can be played with children or among people who don't speak the same language. All you need are sheets of paper (one for each player), pens or pencils, and at least three people gathered together.

PREPARE THE PAPER. Each player holds their paper vertically and folds it into horizontal thirds.

DRAW THE HEAD. In the center of the top third, each player draws a "head." (This doesn't have to be a literal head, though it certainly can be!)

FOLD AND PASS. Fold the top third backward to hide the drawing. Pass the folded paper clockwise to the next player.

DRAW THE TORSO. In the center of the middle third, each player draws a torso.

FOLD AND PASS AGAIN! Fold the paper again so both the head and torso are hidden. Pass the paper clockwise once more.

DRAW THE LEGS OR FEET. In the center of the bottom third, each player draws legs, feet, or any kind of lower appendages.

REVEAL YOUR CORPSE! Unfold the papers to reveal your exquisite creations.

ASSESSMENT AND APPRECIATION

As your collaborative experiments wrap up, take some time with your dream partner to reflect on your journey together. Do you feel closer? Were you able to connect inside the dream realm? If you want to continue this journey together in the future, consider how you might take it further and what else you want to get out of it. Maybe you want to work more on lucid dreaming and dream incubation together, or perhaps you want to collaborate on art; maybe you just want to continue checking in regularly, sharing dreams and insights. Whether or not you choose to continue your partnership, take time to express appreciation for each other and your dreams.

DREAM BIG!

What better way to celebrate your collaborative dreamwork than to host a dream-themed party? Play some surreal games, dress up, and have fun. Encourage people to bring dream-inspired art or music they've made, or a dream they'd like to read aloud. If there's enthusiasm for it, you can plan to put on a dream theater performance of some sort—pitching in to make masks or costumes ahead of time, then acting out or dancing to one another's dreams.

FURTHER READING

The Interpretation of Dreams by Artemidorus

The Committee of Sleep: How Artists, Scientists, and Athletes Use Dreams for Creative Problem-Solving—and How You Can Too by Deirdre Barrett

A Book of Surrealist Games by Alastair Brotchie and Mel Gooding

Big Dreams: The Science of Dreaming and the Origins of Religion by Kelly Bulkeley

50 Secrets of Magic Craftsmanship by Salvador Dali

Rest is Resistance: A Manifesto by Tricia Hersey

The Red Book by Carl Jung

Dreaming Ahead of Time: Experiences with Precognitive Dreams, Synchronicity and Coincidence by Gary Lachman

Dream Witchery: Folk Magic, Recipes and Spells from South America for Witches and Brujas by Elhoim Leafar

The Oracle of Night: The History and Science of Dreams by Sidarta Ribeiro, translated by Daniel Hahn

Dream Reader: Contemporary Approaches to the Understanding of Dreams by Anthony Shafton

An Alphabet for Dreamers: How to See the World with Eyes Closed by Sharon Sliwinski

BIBLIOGRAPHY

Aristotle. *History of Animals.* Translated by D'Arcy Wentworth Thompson. Clarendon Press, 1910.

Cesaire, Suzanne. "1943: Surrealism and Us." In *The Great Camouflage: Writings of Dissent (1941–1945)*, edited by Daniel Maximin and translated by Keith L. Walker. 34–38. Wesleyan University Press, 2012.

Cortázar, Julio. *Cronopios and Famas.* Translated by Paul Blackburn. New Directions Publishing, 1999.

Dickinson, Emily. *Poems by Emily Dickinson: Third Series.* Edited by Mabel Loomis Todd. Roberts Brothers, 1896.

Hughes, Langston. *The Collected Works of Langston Hughes: Volume 1, The Poems: 1921–1940.* Edited by Arnold Rampersad and David Roessel. University of Missouri Press, 2001.

Oppenheim, Meret. Quoted in *Museum of Dreams*. Accessed July 15, 2025. https://museumofdreams.org.

Martuwarra River of Life, Anne Poelina, and Marlikka Perdrisat. "Ancient Wisdom Dreaming a Climate Chance." In *Traditional Knowledge and Climate Change: An Environmental Impact on Landscape and Communities*, edited by Ana Penteado, Shambhu Prasad Chakrabarty, and Owais H. Shaikh, 3–19. Springer Nature Singapore, 2024. https://doi.org/10.1007/978-981-99-8830-3_1.

Shelley, Percy Bysshe. *The Complete Poetical Works of Percy Bysshe Shelley*. Edited by Thomas Hutchinson. Clarendon Press, 1914.

ACKNOWLEDGMENTS

From Fiona:

First and foremost, waves of gratitude to my editor, Melissa, for making another book with me—for your care, depth, and insight in this work. Thank you to my agent, Alyssa Jennette, for believing in me and having my back through the years. Big thanks to everyone at Andrews McMeel who played a part in bringing this dream into reality—what a crew! Above all, thank you, Kathleen, for your beautiful vision and profound talent; your illustrations elevate this atlas to a work of art.

Thank you, Nicholas, for listening to your dreams and following them to Occupy. And thanks for considering my ideas and opinions as they bubble up and foam over, adding your own to the mix. Thanks to my kids, I and O, for your perspectives and playfulness, for bringing so much love and life into my days. Thanks to the McGinns—hope we can all get better at dream-travel so we can exist in two places at once together!

Thanks to my neighborhood park and community garden and all the folks who contribute to its thriving. To Tulio and Cristina and other Gather in the Garden folks, for the care and conversation. Thanks to the library for a quiet place to focus, and for the neighbors I run into there, bringing happy interruptions to that. Thanks to Maggie Queeney of the Poetry Foundation. Thanks to my friends and family for helping me feel supported and connected in a big, dreamy web of love: the Bastressoppenchilds, the Mosers, the Alvarado de Lindgrens, Noah and Elise, Rahnee and Mike, Stephany, Katrina, and all the others who uplift and nourish me through this life.

Thank you to those who've left this plane but who have stayed in touch in dreamland.

*

May we dream worlds of deeper nourishment, care, liberation, and connection together, and may we act every day to bring these dreams to life.

From Kathleen:

Thank you so much to Fiona, not just for trusting me with these illustrations but for the kindness, courage, and thoughtful consideration you bring to everything you do. A huge thank-you to Melissa, our editor, for your insight and keen attention to detail and all your hard work throughout this process. Thank you so much to Alyssa Jennette, my agent, for bringing me to *The Dream Atlas*—your patience and belief in my work is appreciated more than I can express. Thank you to everyone at Andrews McMeel for supporting this dream and making it real.

Thank you to my family, always, forever. Your love and support are everything to me.

ABOUT THE AUTHOR AND ILLUSTRATOR

Fiona Cook is a mother and writer living in Chicago. Her debut book, *The Wheel of the Year: An Illustrated Guide to Nature's Rhythms*, a collaboration with illustrator Jessica Roux, was a *New York Times* bestseller and a Kirkus Best Book of 2023 for middle grade. Fiona is inspired by the magic, mystery, and mischief of our planet Earth and draws from that relationship in her work.

*

Kathleen Neeley is a Tulsa-based artist specializing in relief printmaking and illustration. Her work draws from myth and folklore, personal imagery, and nature.

A NOTE ON THE ILLUSTRATIONS

All of the illustrations in this book are linocuts, a form of relief printmaking in which the negative space of an image is carved away from a linoleum block with sharp blades called gouges. Once carved, the block is coated with ink and pressed onto paper to create a print. These particular illustrations were printed by hand, using a metal spoon and a heavy glass tool called a baren. Think of them as big stamps!

The Dream Atlas: *An Interactive Guide to Dreamwork*

The authorised representative in the EEA is Simon and Schuster Netherlands BV, Herculesplein 96 3584 AA Utrecht, Netherlands. (info@simonandschuster.nl)

Page 120: Excerpt from "Ancient Wisdom Dreaming a Climate Chance" by Dr. Anne Poelina. Reprinted by permission of the author.

Amber Lotus
an imprint of Andrews McMeel Publishing
a division of Andrews McMeel Universal
1130 Walnut Street, Kansas City, Missouri 64106

www.andrewsmcmeel.com

26 27 28 29 30 RLP 10 9 8 7 6 5 4 3 2 1

ISBN: 978-1-5248-8880-0

Library of Congress Control Number: 2025949143

Editor: Melissa R. Zahorsky
Art Director: Diane Marsh
Production Editor: Elizabeth A. Garcia
Production Manager: Tamara Haus

The information and practices offered in this book are for educational purposes only and should not replace professional medical advice, counseling, or therapy. Seek guidance from qualified professionals for personalized support.